Beautiful QUILTS as You Go

Keryn Emmerson

American Quilter's Society

P. O. Box 3290 • Paducah, KY 42002-3290
www.AmericanQuilter.com

Located in Paducah, Kentucky, the American Quilter's Society (AQS) is dedicated to promoting the accomplishments of today's quilters. Through its publications and events, AQS strives to honor today's quiltmakers and their work and to inspire future creativity and innovation in quiltmaking.

EDITOR: HELEN SQUIRE
TECHNICAL EDITOR: CHERYL BARNES
GRAPHIC DESIGN: LYNDA SMITH
COVER DESIGN: MICHAEL BUCKINGHAM

PUBLISHED BY AMERICAN QUILTER'S SOCIETY
IN COOPERATION WITH GOLDEN THREADS.

Library of Congress Cataloging-in-Publication Data
Emmerson, Keryn.
    Beautiful quilts as you go / By Keryn Emmerson.
      p. cm.
    Summary: "Technique for quilting with less stress on your hands and body. Learn how to prepare workspace, choose and mark blocks, and join segments after quilting. Quilt complex quilting designs with the walking foot on your home sewing machine"-- Provided by publisher.
    ISBN 1-57432-890-5
    1. Quilting. 2. Patchwork. I. Title
    TT835.E488 2005
    746.46'041--dc22
              2005021775

Additional copies of this book may be ordered from the American Quilter's Society, PO Box 3290, Paducah, KY 42002-3290; Toll Free: 800-626-5420, or online at www.AmericanQuilter.com.

Dedication

This book is dedicated to my husband, Don, who has always encouraged and supported my quilting and writing obsessions, and who insisted, much against my will, that I learn how to use a computer. I can never thank him enough.

I also want to thank my daughter, Seonaid, and my son, Rhys, for being unpaid secretaries from a very early age, for helping with whatever needed to be done, and for loving and using the quilts that I make them.

Thanks to my father for giving me his love of design, and to my mother for showing me the wisdom of finishing what I start.

Thanks to my twin sister, Meredith England, my best friend and quilting partner, for her never-ending support and advice.

Thanks to Kaye Brown, of The Finishing Touch, for being a good friend and giving me inspiration through the years.

Thanks to Cheryl Barnes and Marcia Stevens for their help and support in the early days of this quilting adventure.

Contents

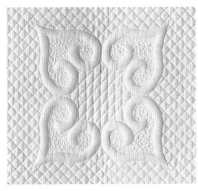

Introduction

Quilting has come into its own in recent years after languishing for decades and being seen merely as an adjunct to patchwork. Now with the rise of machine quilting and the relative ease with which we can accomplish ornate quilting, there is a resurgence in quilting for its own sake. These designs are based on traditional motifs that quilters have used for centuries, but they have been updated for today's methods of quilting. Beautiful results can be achieved by everybody.

Quilt-as-You-Go techniques have been used for many years as a way of finishing quilts without the necessity of using a large frame for hand quilting or having to manage the bulk of the whole quilt when machine quilting. In some cases, the results were less than satisfactory usually because the battings available were hard to work with and the techniques cumbersome. Modern battings are much more stable and easier to work with and give consistently good results. Many techniques have been refined over the years so that today they are a viable alternative to traditional methods of quilting.

QUILT-AS-YOU-GO ADVANTAGES:

- The bulk of the quilt never has to be manhandled through the opening of the machine.

- The small size of the individual pieces makes it possible to quilt complex designs with a walking foot.

- The component pieces of the quilt take up less storage space than a complete quilt during the quilting stage.

- Utilizes every scrap of batting, so there is little or no waste.

- There is no need for a single large piece of backing fabric.

- Minimizes the strain of machine quilting on hands and body, which is an important consideration for those with health problems.

- It is possible to use thicker battings.

- Breaks the quilting process into easily manageable steps, leading to greater enthusiasm and more finished quilts!

- Four Quilt-as-You-Go methods to choose from.

- Perfect for patchwork quilts and creating quilts from vintage blocks.

- Countless possibilities – blocks, strips, or combinations.

Patterns & Projects

Page 26

Beautiful Quilt-as-You-Go patterns and projects are located throughout the book. There are almost 50 handsome patterns suitable for hand or machine quilting, domestic, and home quilting systems. For those professional quilters concerned with copyright issues, the following AQS statement is included.

COPYRIGHT STATEMENT

I am honored that you have chosen to purchase and use my quilting patterns. May my designs make your quilts beautiful!

Keryn

Cover

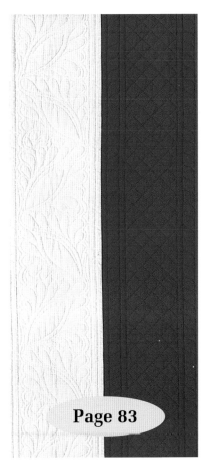

Page 83

Page 86

Chapter 1 — Getting Ready to Quilt-as-You-Go

Setting Up Your Quilting Area

Machine quilting will be more enjoyable if you spend some time setting up your workspace. Often times, the problems associated with quilting are caused by not having the right equipment for the job or not adjusting your working position to eliminate stresses on your body and machine. Without the correct setup you will not enjoy the quilting experience as much as you could.

Table

To arrange your sewing machine properly, you need to have support for the quilt before it reaches the machine and after it leaves the machine. I have two tables set at right angles and an ironing board filling the corner beside me to support the bulk of the quilt. One thing that will really make quilting easier is an extension bed for your sewing machine so that your hands have more room to maneuver the quilt as you follow the pattern.

Chair

An adjustable office chair is another must-have item so that you can sit at the correct height for quilting. I like to sit fairly low for piecing, higher for walking-foot quilting, and higher again for free-motion work. A range of adjustments is ideal but if you do not have an office chair, then you can raise your seating height by placing a telephone book under the cushion on your chair. If you are tall, you may need to lower your chair to obtain the ideal quilting position.

Lighting

It is important to have good lighting in your sewing area to see the marked quilting lines easily and also to see where you have quilted. When free-handing a background design, it's often difficult to see where you have stitched, so some form of side lighting is useful. This highlights the quilted areas so that you can avoid quilting over your previous stitching.

Gathering Your Tools

Basting
- Yellow quilting pins or flower head pins
- Safety pins
- Bulldog® clips
- Wide tape

Measuring/cutting
- Large cutting mat
- Rotary cutter
- Acrylic rulers – 15" square, 6" x 24"
- Metal yardstick

Marking
- Light box
- Golden Threads Quilting Paper
- Markers – water soluble
- Pencils, erasers
- Quilt pounce

Stitching
- Machine quilting needles
- Walking foot
- Free-motion foot

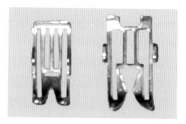

I have modified my quilting feet by cutting out the part directly in front of the needle. This improves visibility around the needle and allows the line to be followed more easily.

Notice that the base plate of the walking foot is detachable, allowing it to be taken off and modified without risking damage to the rest of the foot. I used an old wood chisel to take out the metal in the walking foot and a Stanley® knife to cut the plastic in the free-motion foot. If you do not want to do this yourself, a jeweler can do it; many new quilting feet are designed with these modifications already made.

Please note that the projects and methods in this book have been written for quilting projects using unpieced fabric. Many of the techniques are able to be used on patchwork blocks and strips as well, but when you are learning it is easier to work on plain fabric. Also the need to allow for patchwork's ¼" seam allowances makes some of the techniques difficult to adapt. Try the techniques first, and it will be apparent which ones are adaptable for pieced blocks.

Fabrics

Traditionally quilting fabrics have been cotton, silk, and wool. Today cotton is the most widely available and the most affordable. Choose fabrics with a fine, close weave that will show the stitches well. Sateen is a luxurious looking fabric that can really show off your quilting stitches. Avoid fabrics with a coarse weave as it can make the quilting look distorted.

I like to prewash the fabric I use for strippy quilts and wholecloth quilts. The pieces are quite large and there is no piecing to disguise the effects of shrinkage, so it's better to preshrink. I wash yardage in the washing machine with a gentle, liquid detergent on a short setting to keep fraying to a minimum. I clip the corners and centers of the cut edges to discourage fraying. I often dry yardage in the dryer, which also helps preshrink the fabric.

Pale colored fabrics have different characteristics than darker ones. They are easier to mark and the quilting will show up better. Patterned fabrics can disguise the quilting so that it only shows up in extreme lighting, so bear that in mind when choosing fabrics for your project. I like to use a print fabric on the back to help disguise any imperfections, but I tend to use prints that will still show up the quilting to advantage. Pale prints with scattered motifs are ideal. Look at antique wholecloth and strippy quilts for an idea of what prints work best for quilting.

Choose backings that allow you to use the same thread top and bottom. Many machines do not achieve a balanced quilting stitch and so have bobbin thread appearing on the top or top thread appearing on the back. Avoid this problem by using fabrics that are similar in tone and color so that the same thread can be used top and bottom.

Threads

I use everything on my quilts from cotton wrapped polyester thread to pure cotton, polyester to rayon, monofilament to silk. My main concern is quality; I do not use cheap thread, no matter what it's made of. I use strong thread such as poly and cotton-wrapped poly for everyday quilts which will receive a lot of wear and reserve the more fragile threads such as rayon and fine cotton for quilts that will not be treated as harshly. I have used rayon to good effect when meandering backgrounds; the high density of quilting means that there is less stress placed on the individual stitches.

Choose thread to match the top fabric exactly, or if an exact match is not possible go a shade darker. If you are a confident quilter and you want your stitches to show up dramatically, choose a specialty thread such as a variegated or metallic thread. Meander or freehand backgrounds look great done in these sorts of threads.

When choosing a *variegated thread* for a particular project, it is often a good idea to choose a thread whose colors contrast with the base material. A blue-yellow variegated thread can look fabulous on green fabric or a blue-red on purple fabric. If the fabric does not match any of the thread colors, then there is less chance of the thread appearing to vanish whenever the variegation matches the base fabric. Use a plain thread in the bobbin to match the backing or try a variegated thread in the bobbin as well. If the thread is thick there may be tension difficulties. A thinner variegated may work. New threads are being developed every year. Keep experimenting and trying new threads to find which ones work best for you and your machine.

Wind several bobbins of thread before you start quilting. You will use them all and it helps to keep the flow of quilting going if you do not have to stop and wind bobbins all the time. This sort of quilting is thread intensive especially when you are using the same thread top and bottom, so it pays to buy the larger spools or cones. I often make a serious dent in a 1000-yard spool on one quilt. The thread is often used for the joining process as well, so have enough on hand so that you do not run out. Keep a record of the color number in case you need more thread. Store wound bobbins with the spool of thread in a small press-seal bag.

Battings

There are many battings available now that work well for QAYG. I favor natural fiber battings such as wool and cotton because they are easy to work with and give great results. Polyester battings vary widely in thickness and quality and the thicker ones can be very difficult to control. Thin poly battings may be suitable and ones containing a scrim are usually easier to machine quilt because they are more stable. Check the manufacturer's specifications if you are unsure of the properties of any batting. The specifications will give you valuable information about quilting density and suitable uses.

Many battings can be prewashed to minimize shrinkage. Follow the manufacturer's directions to wash battings. Before I use any batting, I quilt a sample so that I can judge for myself whether I like the results and check that it is easy to use. If you do not know whether you like the effect of shrinkage, make samples using both washed and unwashed batting then wash them as you would wash the finished quilt. Label all samples so that you can refer to them later.

The color of the batting can also be a deciding factor. If you are using very white fabric you may want to choose a white batting. Cream battings can cause a white fabric to look dull. Also, there are black and gray battings available now that can help intensify the colors of the material used in the top—a point to consider if you are making an Amish type quilt with deep-colored fabrics.

It is possible to use two layers of different battings to get a specific result. A thin poly batting over unshrunk cotton will give the effect of trapunto. This is too bulky to quilt normally on the standard machine but is possible using QAYG methods.

Choosing Designs

Everyone has different tastes, and it's important to know what you like and dislike. Try to analyze what it is you particularly like about the quilts that attract you the most. Maybe you love feathers, or geometric Welsh designs, or floral patterns. Once you realize what you like the most, you can start planning your quilts with that in mind.

When choosing a design to begin with, select continuous-line designs that can be stitched with the minimum of breaks. As you get more confident, you can choose more difficult patterns, including ones that require double stitching. Stitching back over the same line of quilting is a skill you should master because then you can machine quilt any pattern you like. Stitch slowly and aim to sew exactly into the holes left by the previous line of stitches.

When choosing designs, keep in mind the finished quilt. The amount of work you put into the quilt varies according to its intended purpose—lots of work for an heirloom quilt, less work for a love-it-to-pieces type quilt. Many of the designs in the pattern section can be stitched with little effort using the walking foot, so they are ideal for most quilts. Some designs are elaborate and will require more work on your part, so use them for special quilts.

Try to keep the designs balanced across the quilt, so that some areas are not more heavily quilted than others. Also it can help to repeat a pattern regularly to help tie the whole quilt together. Look at quilting books and photos of antique quilts and prizewinners at shows to help educate yourself as to what you like best.

When planning a strippy quilt, it is often easier to alternate geometric and flowing designs so that the quilt has a pleasing balance to it. I generally use the geometric design on the darker strips and the flowing design on the lighter strips where it will show up more dramatically. The final choice is up to you and depends on your level of expertise. To begin with, you might choose to have the easily stitched designs on the light fabric and the more difficult ones on the darker one, helping to disguise any mistakes in the quilting. Take your time over the planning stage and try to think of all the possibilities.

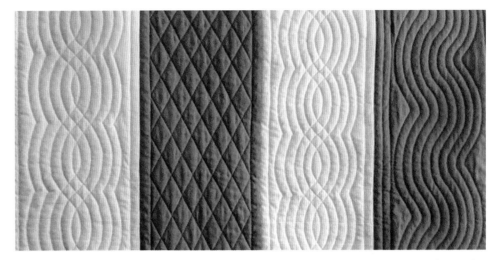

This blue and white strippy was entirely stitched with a walking foot. The patterns on the blue strips include a 60-degree diamond grid, and a wave design, while the white strips are an easy-to-follow cable.

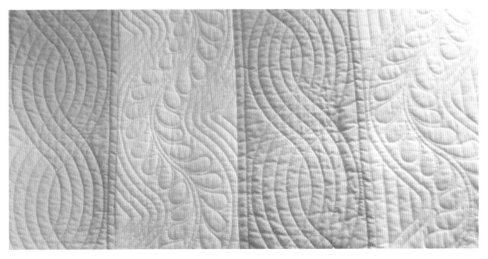

This pink and white strippy uses a cable in the pink strips, stitched with a walking foot, and a feather in the white strips, quilted with the free-motion foot. The backgrounds of the feather strips are quilted in lines to provide contrast with all the curves of the feathers and cables.

Chapter 2 — Keryn's Tips & Quilting Advice

Cutting Tips

Because the pieces to be cut can be quite large, it is helpful to have a large cutting mat. Two 24" mats will give a 48" surface that is adequate for most cuts. Try to use the same brand mat so that they butt up together without any gap. Position the mats on the end of a table so that you can walk around and cut from different directions to avoid having to shift the fabric. A new cutter blade will make cutting the thicker layers easy. Be extra careful to stay in control of the cutter to avoid accidents.

When cutting long lengths of fabric, there will sometimes be two folds in the material. When you double up the fabric layers, it is important to cut at right angles to both these folds to avoid a V shape at the fold. Take plenty of time arranging the fabric to avoid this problem.

Use the square acrylic ruler placed along the fold so that you cut at right angles. Place the metal yardstick next to the acrylic ruler so that an initial cut can be made the whole length of the fabric. Once a clean, straight edge is cut, use the acrylic ruler and move it along the fabric carefully. Before cutting the next strip, use the yardstick to make sure that the cut edge of the fabric is straight; if necessary square up the edge again.

When cutting large squares of fabric or batting, I make two initial cuts, which separate the piece I want from the rest of the material. I prefer to turn the board or walk around the table to make the next two cuts rather than shift the material. This will give a more accurate result.

Batting can be cut in the same way but only folded once; otherwise there is too much thickness beneath the rulers. You may have to lean your body weight on the ruler to keep it from shifting. Squares of batting are best cut as a single thickness. Try cutting samples of batting to see whether you can successfully cut accurate shapes before committing yourself to using it for the whole project.

Marking Tips

Mark your designs before layering and basting your quilt sandwich. There is no one marker that will show up on every fabric, so I use a variety of markers. The main consideration with any marker is how to remove it. Always pre-test any marker so that you know it will wash out when the quilt is finished.

When machine quilting, the marks need to be darker than for hand quilting as the light from the machine tends to make the markings harder to see. Graphite pencil lines are not ideal, except for straight line quilting with the walking foot where the line is always directly in front of the foot and easily visible. I mark grids and straight lines with an F pencil, or with a water-soluble graphite pencil such as Crayola® Aqua Sketch colored pencils, or Portfolio Series™ white to gray drawing pencils.

For detailed, ornate designs stitched with a free-motion foot, I use washable felt pens such as Faber-Castell Connector Pens, or washable Colorific® pens. They need to be fine-tipped so that the line is thin and accurate.

When I buy a set of markers I take a scrap of fabric and write with each marker, giving each color a name, such as leaf green, apple green, or lime green, and write that name with the pen. I keep the pens in the same order as I use them (easy with Connector Pens!). I wash the material and see which pens vanish the most easily. The light blue and green ones seem to go the quickest, then the orange and yellows. The colors that do not wash out completely are pinks, dark blues and purples. They all wash out to pink, so it's important to be able to identify which is which on your sample. Never use a felt pen if you have not tested it first. Take the pens that do not wash out and give them to your children so that they are not in the sewing room anymore.

If you have reservations about using these markers, try a blue washout pen, a Roxanne™ Quilter's Choice chalk pencil, or the marker of your choice. Some other markers to try are General's® Pastel Chalk pencils, and Bruynzeel® chalk pencils.

Light Box
Use a light box when tracing designs onto the fabric. If you do not have a light box, you can improvise one from a household object like a glass chopping board. If you have an extension table, you can open it up and put a sheet of acrylic over the gap or you can use a glass-topped table with a light underneath. A lot of outdoor table settings have glass-topped tables and they're ideal surfaces to work on.

Just make sure that the light does not heat up the tracing surface too much, as some markers become permanent when heated. Have a reasonable distance between the light source and the tracing surface or use a cool globe light.

Draw in any registration lines you will need to help align the pattern in the correct position. These registration lines are often not quilted, so make sure that they are marked with light pressure and with a marker that is easy to remove.

On a strip for a strippy quilt, this will mean marking the center line down the length of the strip, and a starting line at right angles at one end of the strip. If any of the designs you are using are directional, then make sure that you have them facing in the correct direction. For instance, feathers can seem to climb up the strips or face down them. You need to be aware of this as you mark.

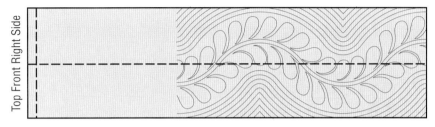

Always mark "top" on the edge of the strip that will be at the top of the quilt so all the strips can be joined correctly. For a block, mark the diagonal, vertical, and horizontal lines through the center of the block.

When tracing, tape the pattern down so you can move the fabric without disturbing the patterns. Hold the fabric steady with one hand and lift the marker often so that it does not drag the material with it. Trace the designs with a light pressure to avoid distorting the fabric and also to minimize ink transfer if using felt-tipped markers.

Whenever you lift the marker, try to keep your hand going in the direction of the line. Often as you lift your hand, it veers off the line and the marker leaves a series of little eyelashes showing. These can be very distracting as you quilt because that little deviation may cause you to quilt in the wrong direction.

Work slowly for accuracy and take frequent breaks. The hand holding the fabric steady will often tire before your drawing hand. Try not to put too much stress on that hand and shake both hands out often. Good music and something warm and soothing to drink will make tracing more enjoyable.

If your drawn line is not accurate, your quilted line probably will not be either! Where possible, overlap the previous markings on the pattern to ensure that the new area to be marked will line up properly. If something does not look right or you are having trouble making things fit, stop and have a good look at what you are doing. Marking should be easy; if it's difficult, then more than likely there is something wrong or out of place. Check measurements and previous lines to see if there is a problem.

Ruler Work

For grids and straight lines, I use several types of rulers to get nice clean lines: small steel rulers, 6" and 12" long, to trace small areas of gridding and a 24" acrylic ruler for larger areas. Make sure that you regularly clean the edges of any ruler you use when drawing on fabric. Ink and pencil residue can transfer to the fabric causing stains. A wipe with a small amount of rubbing alcohol should clean away any build-up.

Stencils

Stencils are another way of transferring patterns to the quilt. If the design I'm using has circles, I use a circle cutter to make an appropriate size stencil so that I can get a good clean line on my fabric.

If a design uses a simple motif repeatedly, it may be easier to make a stencil than to trace each motif. Balance the time it will take to make the stencil against the benefits of having it. Do not spend valuable time making a perfect stencil when there are quicker methods of transferring the design.

Stencils are invaluable when you are marking a dark fabric that you cannot trace through, or when you have already sandwiched the quilt and wish to add another motif.

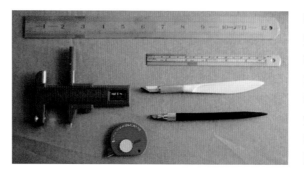

Stencils can be made of anything that you can run the marker against. Plastic and card are more durable than paper stencils but harder to cut. Go for thin, supple plastic so that you can make accurate cuts. Use an Olfa® Touch-Knife, which fits in the hand and is easy to control.

Quilting Paper

Some materials are difficult to mark or you may prefer to avoid marking on your project altogether. I like to use Golden Threads Quilting Paper, a sturdy, lightweight vellum, and trace my design on the paper with a water-soluble marker. Cut and layer up to 15 sheets of paper under the traced copy and needle punch on your unthreaded sewing machine. This will give you multiple copies of the chosen design that can be pinned or spray basted in place, and then quilted through the paper following the stitching path created with the holes. The paper pulls easily away from the stitches and any leftover whiskers can be removed with a sticky lint roller. Try using a pounce box and chalk for fast marking—rubbing the pounce pad over the punched paper is a quick and easy way to transfer your design. Refer to page 31.

Basting Tips

Strips

Clamp one backing strip, right side down, to the edge of a table and tape the other side to the table. Do not place tape or clamps over any registration marks. Place the strip of batting on top. Position the matching top strip on top of the batting, lining up any registration marks, and pin together with long quilting pins through all layers.

To prevent shifting as the piece is quilted, use enough pins so that the three layers are anchored firmly together, but not so many that the quilt bristles with them. Pinning every two to three inches is adequate. To avoid pleats and puckers, try pinning more closely. To save time, try spacing them out a bit more.

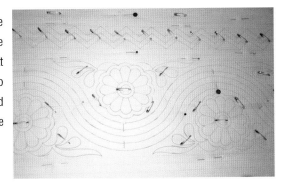

I use long straight pins for much of the basting. Because each piece is completed relatively quickly, the straight pins will be removed early on. They are extremely easy to place and remove, and if you are careful there is little chance of being stabbed or the pins falling out. I use safety pins for areas that will be completed last, or that will require a lot of turning and twisting to complete. Flower head pins are good, as are the yellow-headed quilting pins. All these pins have long shanks to get through the quilt sandwich easily and large heads to help lever the point back up through the layers. Smaller pins hurt the fingers too much and come out too easily.

One-inch safety pins are small enough to quilt around and big enough to manipulate with ease. I store my pins in a wide-mouthed jar and do not bother to do them up. It saves a huge amount of time not having to open every pin before you use it. Never put your hand into the jar—just shake a few pins at a time onto the lid and pick them up as you need them. A small amount of talc powder will help keep them from rusting. A magnetic pincushion is wonderful for collecting unused pins from the quilt.

Place pins in the quilt, trying to avoid the quilting lines. Do not do any safety pins up yet, just place them through all three layers. I spread the fingers of my left hand out and press down to hold the quilt steady, then pin between my first two fingers. I do not want to pull the layers out of place at this stage and if I closed each pin as I went, I'd run the risk of doing so. It's extremely efficient to go back later and close all the pins at once. There is a small tool called a Kwik Klip™ that holds the point of the pins up as you close them, and I would not be without mine. The last thing you need is to prick your fingers and bleed all over your quilt. You can also use the bowl of a spoon to hold the tip of the pin up and away from your fingers. Safety pin the edges together after the tape and clamps have been taken off, one safety pin in between each long pin.

A useful tip to know is that your *own* saliva will remove your blood. If you have an accident with a pin and bleed on your quilt, chew up a small scrap of fabric and use your *own* saliva to blot the blood from the quilt. If you've been drinking coffee, rinse your mouth out with water first!

Blocks

Place the backing square right side down on the table and tape across the corners to hold it securely in place. Place the batting on top aligning the edges. Lay the top fabric on the batting. Tape one corner in place, then position the adjoining corner so that it is directly above the corner. Tape securely across the corner. Repeat until the block is aligned exactly with the backing beneath.

To baste the layers together, pin every 1½" along the edges, placing the pins alternately, and at right angles to the edge. Place pins throughout the block, avoiding the quilting lines where possible. There should be pins every 4" or so.

Be careful when removing tape and do not fray the fabric. Pin corners together aligning all the raw edges carefully. Prepare the other blocks in the same way.

Stitching Sequence

Wherever possible I try to *stabilize* the piece by completing the walking foot work first, which isolates the areas of free-motion quilting and holds all the layers together securely. Most of the pins will be removed by the time the walking foot work is done, making the piece easier to maneuver.

With the walking foot, quilt any straight framing lines on the strip, then any lines that will serve to anchor the strip, such as center lines of cables, spines of feathers, or center lines of crosshatching.

Begin with the walking foot work, as it is the easiest. Quilt the outside lines first, then start on grid lines and stitch all the way to the other end, putting the needle in the fabric and pivoting at corners. It takes practice to sew on the line, and by the time you get to the curved lines, you will be much more experienced.

I like to stabilize each cable strip with the two center lines of quilting before I go on and stitch each line in a strip. This means that even though the quilt is being handled for an extended time, each strip is anchored by those initial lines of quilting. Also it's good therapy to know that you have done some quilting in each area and made a good start. Fill in the other lines gradually. If you're feeling tired, work on the easy lines and do the complex ones when you feel fit. Remember to change thread colors when sewing the contrasting strips.

The trick to quilting curved lines with a walking foot is to sew slowly and move the fabric a little at a time. I do not mind how slowly I go, because I know it's still quicker than hand quilting. Do not put too much stress on the machine by pulling and pushing the quilt; try to work with the machine by moving the fabric gently and evenly. Always stop with the needle down in the fabric, so you can give your hands a rest and rearrange the fabric without shifting the position of the quilt.

Handling the Quilt

By quilting the quilt in sections, the bulk is minimized and the pieces are much easier to control than a full-size quilt. The piece can be folded or rolled to fit through the machine easily and minimize drag on the quilt.

Fold the quilt into a tidy package that is easy to maneuver. Always make sure that the quilt can feed through easily. Sometimes the pins can get hooked on the edge of the table, or you can lean on the quilt and hold it back. What looks like a problem with the foot or the stitch length, can actually be caused by the quilt not being able to move forward freely.

Hold the area in front of the foot flat, and use your fingers to steer the piece so that the needle follows the line exactly. A clear view of the needle is essential.

If there seems to be excess fabric ahead of the foot, lower the needle and lift the foot. Push the extra fabric back under the footplate and carefully lower the foot. You may need to do this several times to distribute the fullness and stitch it down.

Stitch Size

Stitch size is a personal choice, depending on what you personally find pleasing to the eye. It varies from quilter to quilter. Big stitches are weaker than small stitches, as they lie on top of the quilt and get worn away and break. Small stitches are strong, but if they are too small they give a spotty look to the quilting. The ideal is medium length, regular stitches that define the quilting line without being obtrusive.

Burying Your Threads

Different quilting techniques can require different size stitches. I would quilt in the ditch at a normal 2.5 setting, but if I stitched a small, intricate pattern, I would use smaller stitches to help define the curves. Every stitch is straight; curved lines of quilting are just a collection of straight stitches. The smaller the stitch, the smoother the curve. It's important to allow enough stitches in a curving line so that there are no peaks and points.

Threads – Starting and Stopping

With many of the strippy designs, the lines of quilting will start and end on the edges of the strips, meaning they will be caught and held in the construction or binding seams. However, there will be threads to secure in the free-motion motifs, and background fillers, and I tie these off by hand.

Many new machines have a lock stitch, and the bad news is that it's not a good idea to use it. It works by forming a knot of thread on the back, and this knot can wear off over time and then there is nothing anchoring the line of quilting.

I always leave three to four inches of my top and bobbin threads so that I can easily tie them off and bury them in the batting.

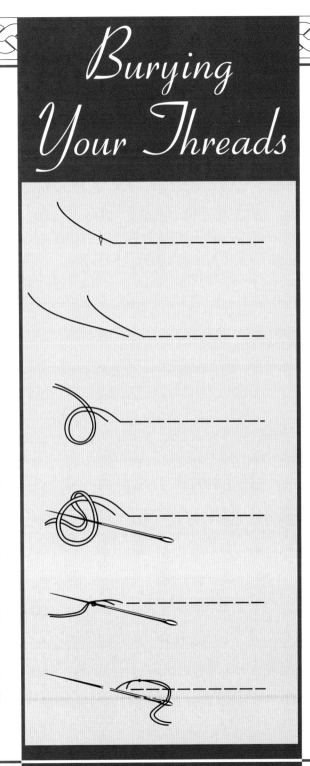

To begin stitching, hold the top thread lightly so that it does not snag underneath and cause a bird's nest on the back. Sew the line of quilting and end off leaving three to four inches of thread, top and bottom.

Return to the beginning and pull gently on the top thread. The bobbin thread will appear and can be brought to the surface. Hold both threads together and make a loop. Then pull the ends through the loop with the self-threading needle. The self-threading needle is super quick to load and saves eye-strain and time.

Place the needle into the loop and hold the needle ¼" away from the start. Pull the threads to make the knot form around the needle, then slide the needle out of the knot.

Thread the needle by pulling each thread into the slot at the top of the eye. It will give a slight clicking sound when the thread is loaded. Use the ends of the thread for this in case the needle cuts the thread by mistake. Pull the needle and thread with the knot through the fabric carefully and snip the tail.

When I'm quilting, I leave threads to be finished off later, when I can sit under a good light, in a comfy chair and watch a movie and relax while I work. However, if I am quilting and will end exactly where I started, I need to finish off as I go so that the last stitch can go exactly into the first stitch. All bobbin threads need to be brought to the surface so that subsequent lines of quilting do not stitch them down.

Quilting Advice

Your patterns will be stitched either with a *walking foot*, or *free-motion foot*, depending on the type of quilting. Straight lines, gentle curves, and most geometric patterns will be quilted with the walking foot. Elaborate, curving patterns are usually stitched with a free-motion foot.

Straight Stitches

For walking foot work, I usually rest my elbows on the table, and this helps take the stress from the neck, shoulders, and upper back. It also steadies your arms and gives greater control of the quilt.

It's important to let the walking foot do what it is designed to do—feed the three layers through evenly. It cannot do this if you are holding the quilt too tightly, trying to control it yourself. The quilt in front of the foot needs to be loose and free so that the foot can take hold of it and feed it through efficiently. Use your hands to make sure that the quilt is lying nice and flat and then merely guide it through.

Sometimes when you quilt across a previous line of quilting, a pleat will form. This problem can be dealt with by pinning with long straight pins. Lay the quilt out flat and place the pins across the intended line of quilting to distribute the bulk of the fullness. If your machine will handle it, sew right across these pins, taking care not to hit one with the needle; if your machine does not like doing this, then slide the pins out just before you sew over them.

Free-motion Quilting

Free-motion quilting is probably the most intimidating part of machine quilting, but it's just a skill to be learned. The only thing that will improve your ability is practice. When beginning free-motion quilting, you may be embarrassed by your obvious lack of skill, but if you hide your mistakes with patterned fabric and matching thread you can still finish quilts while "practicing."

Free-motion quilting is achieved with the use of a *spring-loaded foot* to control the fabric and the feed dogs lowered (or covered) to allow you to move the quilt in any direction. The movement of your hands and the speed of the machine govern the length of the stitches. You will learn to vary these independently to give the results that you want. It may be daunting at first, but becomes second nature in a short time.

The feed dogs are lowered to assist in easy movement of the quilt when free-motioning, but this is not entirely necessary. Some machines use plates to cover the feed dogs but these add height to the bed of the machine and may cause the quilt to stick under the foot. If you cannot drop your feed dogs, then set your stitch length to zero. This means that the feed dogs will only come up and down, with no rotary motion to drag at the quilt. I have often worked for hours without realizing that I have not lowered the feed dogs, and, in cases such as ditch stitching with free-motion, the feed dogs can actually be helpful.

Free-motion quilting is stressful on the hands and you will find it helpful to try one of the many ways of increasing your grip on the quilt. You may want to use rubber gloves or gardening gloves with sticky dots on them. There are knitted cotton gloves with latex dots sold specifically for quilting. You could try rubber thimbles, finger stalls, or latex strapping to

improve your hold. All these accessories aid in relaxing your hands because you will not have to use a lot of force to keep your grip on the quilt. New things are being invented all the time, so keep an eye out for them in magazines and quilt shops.

A machine-quilting horseshoe may help if you have problems maintaining a grip on the quilt. It's shaped like a horseshoe and is placed on the quilt around the foot. Handles on either side allow you to steer the quilt in comfort. They have to be used in conjunction with an extension table and it takes a bit of getting used to, but certainly helps to lessen the stress on your hands.

Sit high enough so that your arms are not resting on the table. In order to move freely, only your hands should touch the table. If you are sitting too low, you will raise your shoulders to try and move your arms, and this will give you headaches, cramps in your back and shoulders, and muscle fatigue. Often a change in height of only an inch or two can give dramatic results. If you are having problems with fatigue while quilting, try this first.

Practice Elements of Free-Motion Quilting

Later in the book you will need squares of pre-quilted fabric to practice the QAYG joining techniques, so it is a good idea to create several sandwiches of fabric and batting and practice free-motion quilting. Very small pieces are harder to control, as your hands have nothing to hang on to, so make 18" square samples. Cover the piece with quilting, and then cut into four squares to use as QAYG samples. If you use a plain fabric, it will be easy to write machine and stitch settings directly onto the samples.

There are three elements in free-motion quilting: the *speed of the machine*, the *speed of your hands* moving the quilt, and *following the line of a pattern*. If you try and master all three at once, it will be intensely frustrating. The easiest one to tackle first is the machine speed.

Machine Speed

Start off by running the machine slowly while learning, and build up to a comfortable working speed as you become more expert. If your machine has a variable speed setting, put it on low to begin with and increase it until you find a speed you like. If you do not have *speed control*, you will need to vary the pressure on the foot control; working barefoot can increase your sensitivity to the foot pedal. Learn to listen to the sound of your machine; it should not sound labored because you are sewing too slowly, and it should not be running so fast that it makes you feel anxious. Try for a nice steady hum.

Moving the quilt under the needle is like moving a piece of paper under a pencil. Move both hands together in parallel. Do not turn the quilt like a steering wheel as you stitch, as this increases the chances of puckers and pleats. It may help to keep your thumbs together in front of the foot.

Hand Movement

Begin with easy loops and meanders, concentrating on letting the machine stitch around the curves; do not hurry the movements around the top and bottom of the curves or you will end up with pointy peaks that are ugly. Another easy way to practice is to *write your name* with quilting; you can stitch back along lines wherever necessary and you'll get good practice changing direction and making different size loops. Remember, the ideal is medium length, regular stitches that define the quilting line without being obtrusive.

Many sewing machines have trouble forming the stitches in free-motion quilting, and a look at the back will show the bobbin thread pulled tight and the top thread dragged through. Often times it will consistently occur in the same area of a curve. This can be lessened by stitching smoothly and in time with the machine and making sure that you are not hurrying through that part of the curve. While stitching your first samples, concentrate on getting the stitches even and the lines smooth and curving evenly. Often times, tension problems vanish as you become more practiced.

If you are ready to free-motion on a real quilt, and there are still tension problems, then you can try several things. Only change one thing at a time though, so that when something works you know what was responsible for the improvement.

- Keep your hand movements steady in all directions.

- On the back, "eyelashes" are nearly always caused by extra top thread being drawn through to the back of the quilt.

- Try tightening up the top tension. Take the tension dial numbers higher, or if you have multiple thread guides on your machine, thread them all.

- Loosen the bobbin tension slightly. Hint: righty-tighty, lefty loosey.

Following the Line

When you have practiced the movement of free-motion quilting, you can draw lines and try to follow them. Begin by drawing a large meander and following that. It's far more important to keep the flowing curve of a line rather than to follow the mark exactly; the mark will wash away and no one will know whether you deviated from it so long as the curve is still pleasing. If you constantly hop back to the line in a series of zigzags it will look horribly uneven. If you miss the line just plan to curve back and meet it again as soon as possible. When you've stitched the line, you can echo it either side, just for a bit of practice.

To help you regulate your straight stitch length, try quilting free-motion beside a line stitched at 2.5 with the walking foot. Try to match it stitch for stitch. This is the largest stitch that you are likely to use in quilting.

Practice the design you will be stitching on samples until you feel more confident. At some stage, just take a deep breath and quilt on the actual quilt. Start with a small motif that can be quickly completed. If you are horrified at your first effort, unpick it. Do it again. If you get discouraged, quilt a motif with the walking foot this time. Keep practicing. Do not give up. Do not be so critical!

Not all the quilting on each piece needs to be completed at once. If you are quite comfortable stitching with the walking foot and not yet happy with your free-motion skills, then concentrate on doing the walking foot work first and keep on practicing your free-motion skills. Many patterns have a combination of the two types of quilting so you can be making progress while you are learning.

When quilting you can travel unnoticeably from one area to another by stitching in the ditch of neighboring patches, or by echoing closely another line of quilting. From a distance, these areas of double stitching will be difficult to detect.

Highlights

Different quilting techniques can require different size stitches. Use smaller stitches to help define curves, and allow enough stitches in a curving line so that there are no peaks and points.

All bobbin threads need to be brought to the surface so that subsequent lines of quilting do not stitch them down.

There are three elements in free-motion quilting: the speed of the machine, the speed of your hands moving the quilt, and following the line of a pattern.

When moving the quilt under the needle, do not turn the quilt like a steering wheel as you stitch; this increases the chances of puckers and pleats.

Practice writing your name with quilting; stitch back along lines wherever necessary and you'll get practice changing direction and making different size loops.

When free-motion quilting, it's far more important to keep the flowing curve of a line rather than to follow the mark exactly; the mark will wash away and no one will know whether you deviated from it so long as the curve is still pleasing.

Continuous quilting does not mean non-stop quilting. You need to stop often and shake out your hands, stretch your back and neck, breathe deeply for a few breaths, and focus on something on the far side of the room to relax your eyes. Plan to stop at a point or intersection of the pattern so that when you start again, any small inconsistency is not as noticeable as in the middle of a curve. Do not try to move the quilt straight away; it's better for the needle to go back into the same hole for the first stitch, while you get the fabric under control. There's nothing more annoying than the first stitch being a shocker that has to be pulled out.

Do not sew beyond the limit of control of your hands. If your fingers are slipping off the edge of the machine, then stop and reposition both hands before you continue to quilt and make a mistake. Also, be careful of moving one hand at a time; what usually happens is that the other hand pulls the fabric off course and jagged stitches result. Keep your hands moving in unison.

If you have a lot of similar motifs to quilt, break the boredom by doing other things every three or four motifs. I also make charts on my whiteboard or chalkboard with a circle for every motif I have to stitch. Every time I finish a motif, I get to cross it off the board in a different color. If I'm doing a marathon quilting session, I put the board on the other side of the sewing room so that I have to get up regularly and walk over to it. That way I get to stretch and move around which helps avoid muscle problems.

Chapter 3 Quilt-as-You-Go Techniques

QAYG

There are many QAYG techniques giving different results for different situations. The projects in this book concentrate on several easy methods using a combination of hand and machine sewing. Due to the different construction methods used for QAYG, there usually has to be some hand sewing to make the joins unnoticeable. Use whatever method you feel most comfortable with, and the one that gives you the effect you are after.

Before you start on a project, it is a good idea to *make a sample* of the joining technique so that you are familiar with the methods. Write on the sample any adjustments you made, such as needle settings, stitch length, and thread tensions. It is invaluable to be able to refer back to these samples later.

Use the same standard of materials that you would use in your quilts. Do not be tempted to make your samples out of shoddy fabric, cheap batting, and poor quality thread. Often times these inferior materials will cause extra problems and give unsatisfactory results, and you will not know if your sewing is to blame or the poor quality materials.

Because quilting distorts the material and causes shrinkage, it is vitally important to *measure pieces accurately*. There is a lot of work involved in the preparation of these projects, but that is more than compensated for by the ease of quilting and the impressive results.

	BEAUTIFUL QUILT-AS-YOU-GO TECHNIQUES	
Methods	**Advantages**	**Disadvantages**
Seaming & Binding	- Simple method, easy to do - No calculations or extra fabric allowances - Nothing showing on quilt top - Good for patchwork pieces - Each piece quilted separately	- Seam is bulky and resists lying flat - Noticeable on the back - Binding strip on back adds to bulk - Must be sewn by hand
Sew and Flip	- Extremely simple - Easy to calculate pieces - Unnoticeable on top and back - Can be done entirely by machine	- Quilt piece grows with every addition - Gets heavier and harder to handle as it is quilted - Batting in seam can be bulky
Zigzag & Coverstrips	- Easy to do - Can be done completely by machine - Coverstrips can be designed to look like sashing	- Every seam is noticeable - All sashes must line up correctly
Flat Fold Seams	- Invisible on front, hard to detect on back - Strips are quilted individually - Very easy to manipulate strips - No seam bindings or coverstrips needed	- Back requires hand sewing to be unnoticeable on front - Needs accurate measuring and marking

Seaming and Binding QAYG Method

The quilted blocks are treated like normal patchwork and joined with a single ¼" seam through all the layers, including a 1¼" binding strip in the seam. The seam allowances are forced over to one side and the binding strip sewn down to cover the seam allowances.

This seam needs to be sewn with the walking foot to handle the bulk. If you can move the needle on your machine, adjust it so that it is sewing ¼" from the edge of the right edge of the foot. If you cannot adjust the needle position, choose a spot on the foot to guide along the edge of the quilt to give you an approximate ¼" seam. This is not a seam that lies flat easily, and the layers may need to be trimmed to reduce the bulk. It's one of the easiest methods though, and with a thin batting it can work well.

Sew a Sample

Take two 9" squares of prequilted fabric, quilted right up to the edges. Place together, right sides together. Pin a 1¼" binding strip along the edge through all the layers, making sure all raw edges are lined up exactly. Sew with a ¼" seam. Trim batting as shown in the diagram (fig. 3–1).

Fold coverstrip to the stitching line, then push folded edge over raw edges and stitch to the next block (fig. 3–2). Natural battings such as wool and cotton can be gently ironed to flatten the seam.

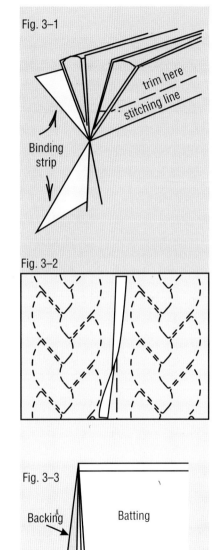

Fig. 3–1

trim here
stitching line
Binding
strip

Fig. 3–2

Fig. 3–3

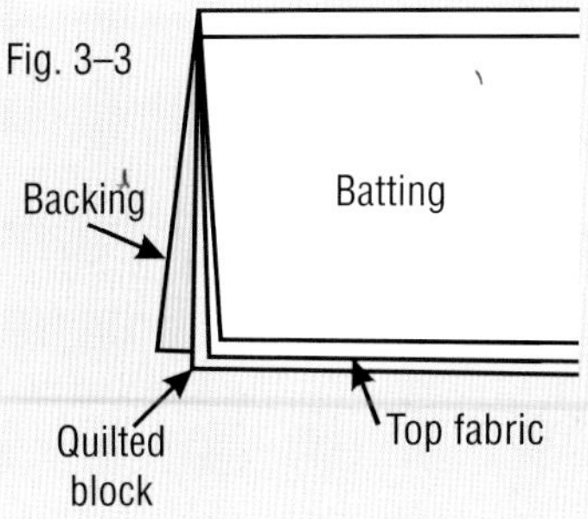

Backing   Batting

Quilted   Top fabric
block

Sew and Flip QAYG Method

The quilted part of the quilt is layered between the top and backing fabric, with the batting on top. All are sewn together with a regular seam, then the layers are folded out to enclose the batting. This can be used to join individual blocks, piecing sections of the quilt, or to add borders. It's ideal to make strippy-style quilts, medallion quilts, or row-by-row quilts. The pieces to be joined are cut the desired size plus seam allowances where required. You will need to cut each piece from the top, batting, and backing.

Sew a Sample

Take a 9" square of prequilted fabric, quilted all the way up to the edge. Next cut a 9" square from backing and top fabric, and one from batting. Arrange the layers as follows: on the bottom, the backing fabric right side up; the quilted block right side up; the top fabric, wrong side up; then the batting.

Pin all six layers together and stitch. I use the edge of my walking foot as a seam guide, because it's roughly ¼" from the edge to the needle. If the distance is greater on your machine, move the needle closer to the edge of the foot if possible, or choose a spot on the foot to guide along the edge of the quilt to give you an approximate ¼" seam (fig. 3–3).

Fold the layers back from the quilt. The batting will be sandwiched between the top fabric and the backing. Pin the outside edges together and run a line of stitching all the way around to hold the raw edges together. A line of quilting ¼" away from the joining seam will encourage the seam to lie flat (fig. 3–4). Quilt as desired.

If you find the bulkiness of this method unappealing, the batting can be attached with a zigzag stitch. Cut the batting piece ½" narrower than the fabric pieces. The batting will not lose any width in the seam, as the fabric will, so it needs to be smaller than the fabric.

Arrange the layers as follows: on the bottom, the backing fabric right side up; the quilted block right side up; then the top fabric. Seam the two fabric pieces in place with the normal ¼" seam. Then zigzag the batting to the raw edges of the seam, taking care not to catch the bottom fabric in the seam. Fold the fabric layers over the batting to cover it. A line of quilting ⅜" away from the seam will hold the batting even more securely. This gives a very flat seam.

Zigzag and Coverstrip Method

The edges of the quilt blocks are butted together and joined with a wide zigzag. On the back, the raw edges are covered with a small coverstrip. On the front, the raw edges are covered with a wider coverstrip, hiding the previous stitching.

Interesting effects can be achieved using stripes as coverstrip sashing. Border prints can often be used to give a

Fig. 3–4

Fig. 3–5

Fig. 3–6

sophisticated effect without a lot of effort (fig. 3–5). Often a wide border print will have smaller stripes printed with it, and if only the wide border is wanted these smaller stripes can add a touch of class to the back or front of any quilt.

Sew a Sample

Cut two 9" squares of prequilted fabric quilted all the way up to the edges. Take the prequilted squares and butt two edges together. Zigzag with a wide, long stitch. This can be done with the walking foot or with a normal foot. If you use a walking foot make sure that the swing of the zigzag stitch will not be greater than the opening in the foot, or a broken needle will result. Set the stitch width to 5 so that it takes a good bite of each square. The stitch length should be around 2.5. Keep the edges of the square pressed together so that there will not be any gaps in the seam. Back tack at the beginning and end to secure the threads.

Back Coverstrips

For the back coverstrip, cut a strip of fabric 1½" wide by 9" long. For the sashing, cut a contrasting strip of fabric 2¾" wide and 9" long. On the back apply a narrow coverstrip over the raw edges of the squares. You will need to turn under both edges of the coverstrips. Use a narrow appliqué zigzag, width 1.5 and length 2.5. Center the raw edges underneath the coverstrip over the zigzagged seam (fig. 3–6).

You can use bias-tape makers to make small folded bindings, or use the old dressmaker's trick of placing pins in your ironing board as guides for pressing the binding strip. Glass headed pins will not melt if the iron happens to touch them.

Front Coverstrips

On the front, apply a wider strip so that all previous stitching is hidden. Both sides of the sashing are stitched in place, using the same appliqué zigzag used to stitch the coverstrip on the back.

Cut a piece of freezer paper 2" wide and at least 9" long. Iron it to the back of a 2¾" sashing strip. Using the tip of the iron, press the extra fabric over the edge of the freezer paper. Turn the strip over and iron to set the folds, then remove the paper and press again.

Apply the prepared coverstrip to the top (fig. 3–7). Fold the strip in half without making a heavy crease. Line the fold up with the middle of the zigzag seam between the blocks. Take out and align the marks with the seam intersections. Pin in position using long straight pins, placing the pin into the lower part of the sashing strip, and up through all layers, leaving the top half free to pull off the point of the pin (fig. 3–8).

Unfold the strip, and pin the free edge to the adjacent block. Stitch both sides in place using a long narrow zigzag stitch and thread to match the sashing (fig 3–9).

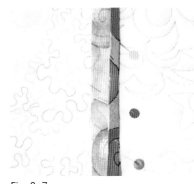

Fig. 3–7

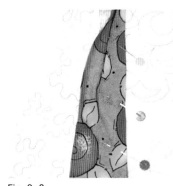

Fig. 3–8

Fig. 3–9

When joining pieces, make sure that:
• the pieces to be joined are the same size
• the edges are kept straight
• the beginning and end of the pieces line up exactly

If the pieces are very long, lay them out on a table so that they are in the correct position and draw marks across the seam so that you can align them properly as you stitch them together.

This is a wonderful method of joining, easy, accurate, and a great finished product. I first heard of this method from Queensland, Australia, tutor Lynne Booth.

Coverstrip Variations

Coverstrips are used to hide the raw edges on the quilt. What sort of strip depends on the effect you want and the method of joining, whether zigzagged or seamed. The coverstrips can be incorporated in the joining seams, or added separately afterwards. They can masquerade as sashing strips on the front, or as camouflage by using the same fabric as the blocks or backing. Using stripes as coverstrips can also add extra interest to the finished quilt. The coverstrips can be cut on the straight or bias grain of the fabric—plaids work extremely well cut on the bias. The extra stretch in the bias strip means it will not distort the quilt if accidentally pulled tight when applying.

For Single Layer Seamed Coverstrips, use a strip of fabric 1½" wide. Sew along zigzagged seams with a seam wide enough to cover the zigzag stitching, fold under the raw edge, and sew to the adjacent block (fig. 3–10 and 3–12).

Try Double Layer Seamed Coverstrips, if you do not like turning under the raw edges of small coverstrips that have been sewn in place. You can use a double-fold binding strip. The strip is folded in half lengthwise and the raw edges are seamed to the zigzagged edge of the blocks, leaving the folded edge free to sew to the adjacent block or strip (fig. 3–11 and fig. 3–12). I personally like this method—it's quick and easy, and I like the added thickness of binding material. Sometimes a zigzagged seam can show as a dent in the finished quilt, and this coverstrip helps to prevent that. Start with a 1½" strip and experiment to find the size strip that you desired.

Make stitched samples of different width coverstrips, so that you can actually see what they look like. Join together any practice sample of machine quilting to experiment with the different techniques. Remember, if the coverstrip is added in the seam it will not necessarily be centered over that seam after it is folded to one side. When joining rows of blocks, the coverstrip may not line up exactly unless you take care to plan for it. Experimenting will allow you to sort out problems like this.

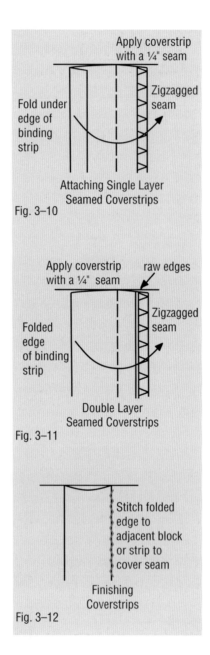

Apply coverstrip with a ¼" seam

Fold under edge of binding strip

Zigzagged seam

Attaching Single Layer Seamed Coverstrips

Fig. 3–10

Apply coverstrip with a ¼" seam — raw edges

Folded edge of binding strip

Zigzagged seam

Double Layer Seamed Coverstrips

Fig. 3–11

Stitch folded edge to adjacent block or strip to cover seam

Finishing Coverstrips

Fig. 3–12

Stitching Variations

The coverstrips can be attached very easily by hand or machine. Several types of machine stitches can be used to secure the strips; all will give a different effect, either hidden or decorative. If a decorative stitch is used, it should be used on both sides of the strip.

Blind stitch – Set the blind stitch so that the swing stitch is very small. The straight stitching should be on the block, and the swing stitch should just catch the edge of the strip. Some machines will do a smaller blind stitch if the stitch is mirrored. Use a thread that matches the block fabric. Monofilament thread will help hide the stitches.

Zigzag – Use a normal stitch length and the smallest width that you can manage. You should be able to stitch one stitch on the block and one on the strip; if you keep missing the strip, you may need to increase the width slightly. Use a thread that matches the strip, or monofilament. Try a zigzag setting of 1.5 width and 2.5 length.

Straight stitch – This is appropriate on '30s style quilts, which often use this as an appliqué stitch. Aim to keep the stitching close to the edge and even. Thread should match the strips for the best results, but some early appliqué was done entirely with white or cream threads.

Blanket stitch – Again, this is good for '30s quilts, as a lot of appliqués from this time were blanket-stitched. Black, red, or camel thread can be very decorative.

Featherstitch – This embroidery stitch will add to the decorative effect. It should be stitched half on the coverstrip and half on the block.

I actually write on the sample with a permanent pen making a note of strip width, seam width, and stitch settings on the machine. That way the information is always available.

Flat Fold Seam Method

This method is suitable for strippy quilts. It depends on a line of quilting 1" in from the edge of the strips, so is not always suited for joining quilted or patchwork blocks. The strips are joined with a ½" seam, leaving the backing on one piece free. The seam batting is removed from one piece, then the backing is turned under and slipstitched to the adjacent block to cover the raw edges.

Sew a Sample

We will join three pieces together, and trial two methods of sewing down the backing. Cut four 9" squares of fabric, and two of contrasting fabric. Cut three 9" squares of batting. Take two squares of the first fabric, and one of the contrasting fabric to make the front of the samples. Mark a 7" square centered on each square of fabric so that it is 1" from the cut edges (fig. 3-13). Mark a square on point inside the lines. These are the quilting lines (fig. 3-14).

On the three remaining squares, mark lines ½" in from all the edges on the back side—these are the backings for the front pieces. Mark the center point of each side on each

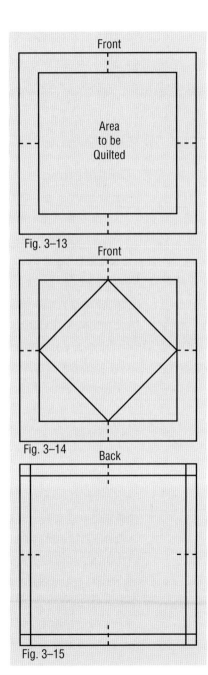

Fig. 3–13

Fig. 3–14

Fig. 3–15

square. On the right side of the contrasting backing square, draw lines ½" in from all edges (fig. 3–15).

Layer the backing, batting, and top squares. Pin corners and centers to prevent shifting, and quilt the design on each one.

Take the contrasting quilted square and on opposite sides, remove the batting beyond the last line of quilting. Pin the top layer of fabric to a quilted square, matching corners and midpoints of sides. Sew on the drawn line, ½" in from the edge. Machine sew raw edges together with a line of basting stitches ⅛" from the edges. Trim the seam to a fraction under ½".

Press under the free edge of the backing fabric, using the ½" line as a guide. Lay the quilt on a flat surface and pin the folded edge of the backing to the stitching of the seam, covering all raw edges. Place the pins vertically to make hand sewing the edge easier. Slipstitch the folded edge to the top fabric by the joining seam, taking care to keep the seam flat and straight.

Another method is to join the other square to the opposite side in the same manner, except the backing fabric should only be folded under ⅜". Tack the fabric in place, overlapping the seam stitching on the back. On the front, ditch-stitch the seam, quilting through the folded backing underneath. This is not as unobtrusive as the hand sewing, but it is quicker and stronger.

Quilt-as-You-Go Block Projects

Zigzag and Coverstrip Method
Wallhanging

Fabric, thread & batting

When you choose the fabric, remember that you will have to trace the design on it. On most pale fabrics, the pattern will show through without a light box. If you choose a dark fabric, you will need an extremely good light box. If you do not have one, ask if your quilting shop has one that you can use. Also bear in mind that quilting will not show up as readily on dark fabric.

Requirements

- 6½ yards of 42" wide fabric—This is enough for the top and back, a hanging sleeve and the binding, plus some to use as a practice square.
- 1⅓ yards of material for sashing. Special effects can be achieved by using vertical stripes, but extra care will need to be taken if you choose to do this.
- 500 yards of thread to match the main fabric, and 100 yards of thread to match sashing if it is different from the main thread color.
- Specialty threads if you choose. I meandered the backgrounds of two blocks using a variegated pastel thread that was very effective.
- 1½ yards of 90" wide batting of your choice. Polyester batting will be harder to handle than a natural batting such as wool or cotton.

Notions

- Blue washout pen or marker. Always pretest marker. *Never iron markings.*
- Masking tape
- Walking foot and free-motion foot if you intend to meander quilt
- Machine-quilting needles
- Self-threading hand-sewing needles or any large-eyed sharp needle
- Large acrylic rulers: 6" x 24" and 15½"
- Sewing supplies, rotary cutter, pins, scissors, seam ripper, etc.
- Long, large-headed pins such as Flower Pins are extremely useful.
- Freezer paper 45" long

Preparing the fabric

The fabric can be prewashed if desired. I always wash muslin because it has a high shrinkage rate, but the better quality materials often have minimal shrinkage. It's best to wash it if you have any doubts at all. I do like to pre-wash my natural fiber batting, because I think the quilt can look rather flat and "empty" when the batting shrinks. Always follow the manufacturer's instructions when washing batting. If you like the crinkled antique look, then you must not prewash cotton battings, as it is the shrinkage that causes that look.

Iron the fabric to remove any wrinkles. Adding starch at this stage will restore some crispness to the fabric if it has been washed.

Cutting

On plain fabric, weaving imperfections or marks are often visible so check for any of these before you begin cutting. Choose to cut the main squares of fabric from the material that has the least of these flaws. Using the other side of the material can minimize these as well.

Fabric

Cut six 2½" binding strips from the width of the fabric. For the hanging sleeve, cut two 9" strips from the leftover fabric, join, and trim to give a piece 56" long.

From a double layer of fabric, cut nine 15½" squares. You will probably only get one pair of squares from the width of the fabric. Cut these squares close to the selvage so that the remainder of fabric can be used for other pieces. Do not include selvages in these squares. Mark the top left-hand corner of each top square with a small number, flip back the corner, and mark the square underneath with the same number. When layering the blocks later, match these numbers so you can be sure the grain is running the same way on both layers.

For the *borders*, cut eight strips 7" x 54" from the length of the fabric. You can cut two strips from the length leftover from cutting the squares.

Cut 1½" *coverstrips* from the length of the leftover fabric to total 354". From the length of the *sashing* material, cut eight 2¾" strips.

Batting

For the *borders*, cut four strips 7" x 56" with the long side along the 90" width of the batting, and nine 15½" squares for the *blocks*.

Marking

If you have ever used your rulers to draw lines with an ink or solvent marker, there will be a residue along the edge of the ruler. This will transfer to the quilt if you use a blue pen. Check the edges of all your rulers and clean them with rubbing alcohol if they are dirty.

Tape the patterns to the table or light box, and position the fabric over them. Align the diagonal lines on the pattern with the lines on the fabric. Hold the fabric to keep it in position and carefully trace all the marks of the design. If there is gridding or linework in the background, mark this next. I use the 24" ruler and an F pencil, or an HB pencil on light fabrics. These leave a very fine, drawn line. Begin marking from the diagonal lines first drawn.

If you wish to meander quilt the background, no marking is necessary. The feather wreath surrounded by echo quilting was not marked either. I simply used the edge of my walking foot as a guide along the previous line of quilting.

You can choose to use the same background filler in all blocks, or do as I did and stitch a sampler of different patterns. I did four with meandering, one with echo quilting, and four with linework (diagonal, chevron, diamond, gridlines, etc.)

This is a good time to practice that free-motion work, but if you do not feel confident enough, all the backgrounds can be done with echo quilting or linework. Attach the walking foot to the machine according to the manufacturer's directions.

Quilting

Make a practice sample from leftover fabric and stitch some samples so that you can choose the best settings for your machine. It may be helpful to set the stitch length shorter so that there are more stitches per inch. This will produce smoother curves and will make it easier to maneuver the quilt, as the foot will not be feeding the material through so quickly.

Quilt ¼" from the edge around the block to anchor the layers, making sure the edges of all three layers are exactly aligned. Quilt the designs following the stitching diagrams. Leave 3" to 4" thread tails so that you can end them off as explained on page 15.

Quilt slowly and carefully, especially on curved lines, and lift the foot often to allow the quilt to be shifted in the direction you are quilting. Always anchor the work by

Fig. 4–1

stopping with the needle down in the fabric. If it seems like hard work, just remember how long it would take by hand or how hard it would be with the free-motion foot. You'll soon feel better!

End off the threads before stitching the background fillers. Then quilt the middle line of the background lines in each corner working from the center out to the edge. Finally complete all the background quilting lines. End off all the threads.

To trim the blocks, measure all the blocks with the square ruler to find the smallest size. Quilting shrinks and distorts the blocks so that they need trimming to a uniform size afterwards.

Trim all the blocks to the smallest measurement, keeping the design centered (fig. 4–1). If you need to trim the blocks to 15", then the 7½" lines on the ruler should be positioned so that they run through the center of the quilted design. Check that the 15" lines of the ruler are still on the block, not angling off the edges. Trim the top and right-hand side, turn the block, and repeat to trim the remaining two sides. This time, the 15" line will be on the exact edge of the block.

From this point on, I cannot give exact measurements, as your blocks may have been trimmed to a different size from mine. You will need to measure your work as you progress.

Strips and Borders

Sashing Strips

A simple way to cover the joins with sashing strips is to cover the short joins first, then run the long sashing strips through. However, I used another method to get the particular effect I wanted, as the floral print in my quilt is actually a stripe. I did not want the intersections of the sashings quilted down by the applique stitches. If this is not something that applies to your quilt, just follow the instructions but cover the short joins first not bothering about the pointed ends, then apply the long sashes (fig. 4–2).

Cut a piece of freezer paper about 2" wide and 45" long. Position it carefully on the wrong side of a sashing strip, shiny side down, so that there is about ¼" of fabric showing either side. Iron in place. Fold the fabric over the edge of the long sides of the paper and iron to give a nice crisp fold. Repeat for the other side. Remove the paper and press carefully again.

Join the blocks into three rows of three. Apply narrow coverstrips to the back to hide the raw edges. Join two rows together and cover the long seam on the back with a narrow coverstrip. Measure the quilt on the front and note the distance between edges and seam intersections. Mark these points on both sides of the prepared sashing strip.

Apply the prepared sashing strip to the top. Fold the strip in half without making a heavy crease, line the fold up with

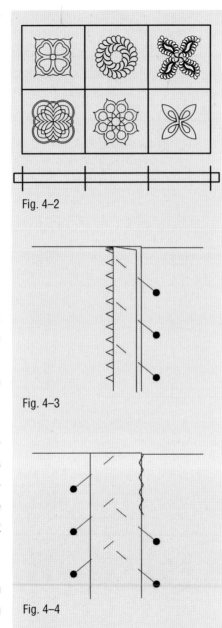

Fig. 4–2

Fig. 4–3

Fig. 4–4

the middle of the zigzag seam between the blocks, and align the marks with the seam intersections. Pin in position using long straight pins, unfold the strip, and pin the free edge to the adjacent block. Stitch both sides in place using a long narrow zigzag stitch and thread to match the sashing (fig 4–3).

Join the other row of three blocks to the quilt and apply the coverstrip and sashing strip in the same fashion (fig. 4–4).

To cover the remaining seams on the front, start by cutting a sashing strip as long as the block measurement plus 1".

At one end, mark a 45-degree line on the wrong side of the material. Fold in half lengthwise, right sides together, and sew on the line.

Trim the seam allowance at the point and turn right side out, opening seam allowances to distribute the bulk.

Press the edges of the strip over the freezer paper to give a nice crisp fold. Remove paper. Place the sash in position on the quilt, centered over the seam and the point lying over the previously attached sashing. Mark the place where the small sash crosses the next line of sashing. Draw a 45-degree line through that point on the wrong side of the material. Fold the strip in half, right sides together, and sew on the line. Trim the seam allowance at the point and turn right side out, opening seam allowances to distribute the bulk.

Re-press edges, then appliqué in place. Only the two center sashes will need points on both ends; the others will extend all the way to the edge of the block. I did not appliqué the points down until all the sashes were in place so I could position them pleasingly.

Frame Borders

The borders are joined into a frame, sandwiched with frames of batting and backing cut the same size, quilted as one piece, and then zigzagged to the body of the quilt with coverstrips over the joins front and back. Accurate measuring is necessary, and it's rather cumbersome, but it can give good results. The main advantage is that the frame is quite maneuverable on its own, allowing it to be quilted with a walking foot.

The quilting will cause the border to shrink somewhat, so an extra ¾"–1½" in length is added. Do not make the mistake of allowing too much extra, though; if it does not shrink as much as expected, the hole in the middle will be too large for the body of the quilt. It's better to cut the opening larger after quilting.

Border quilting patterns that have a specific design for the corner will be marred by a mitered seam line, so butt-joint the seams, as this will place the seams in an inconspicuous area of the corner.

Calculate the length required for the border strips by adding together the length of the joined blocks, plus the 7" width of the border, plus ½" for seam allowance, plus the amount you want to allow for shrinkage. In this quilt, 1" was allowed (8½" total).

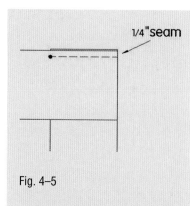

¼" seam

Fig. 4–5

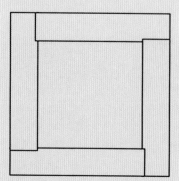

Fig. 4–6

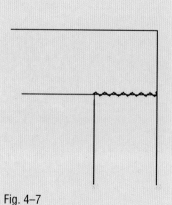

Fig. 4–7

Overlap the ends of the border as shown in fig. 4–5 and sew together with a ¼" seam. An extra ¼" is allowed for in the seam allowance so that the borders will end up the same size as the batting frame, which has butted seams instead.

• Repeat with the other corners to make a frame.
• Press the seam so that both strips lie flat.
• Make a frame of the backing pieces in the same manner.

The batting measurement will be ½" shorter because there are no seam allowances to take into consideration. The strips are butted together and joined with a large zigzag stitch (fig. 4–6). Join the batting into a frame with butt joints in the opposite direction to the top and back so that the seams of all the layers do not lie on top of one another. Careful marking of alignment points is the key to success (fig. 4–7).

Measure the outside edges of all three frames to make sure that they are all the same size. Fold each side in half and mark the centerline on both edges. Mark the quarter lines as well on both sides of the centerline. Continue these lines across to the other side of the strip. Mark all the sides of all the layers in the same way. When the layers are pinned together, all these marks will be aligned ensuring that the layers are in the right place.

The quilting design needs to be traced onto the border frame at this stage. If you do not intend to meander the background of the border, you will need to mark parallel lines across the borders to balance out the density of quilting. Bind to complete – enjoy!

Layer the backing, batting, and border together, aligning the marks and pinning the edges together with the pins at right angles to the edges. Using the walking foot, baste the edges together with a line of stitching ¼" from the edge. Tape each side to the table, one at a time, so that it lies nice and flat. Place pins throughout the design to hold all the layers in place.

Quilt the design. When using the walking foot, you do not have to turn the whole frame, just swivel the portion you are working on. Finish quilting the background filler design. End off threads.

Measure the opening in the frame on all sides. Compare to the measurement of the body of the quilt. The blocks need to fit into the frame exactly. Trim the inner edges of the frame to fit if necessary. The opening in the frame should not be too large, because only one inch was allowed for the shrinkage caused by quilting. However, if it is wider than the body of the quilt, more background quilting could be added to shrink it further or a small strip of batting attached to bring it out to size.

Finishing the Edges

When the border and quilt fit together well, draw lines across the seam so that the edges can be stitched together in the correct alignment. Zigzag the border to the quilt, one side at a time, lining up the marks. Check to see that the complete quilt lies flat when finished. Sometimes the stitching will need to be released, the area realigned, and the stitching redone.

Cover the seams on the back with narrow coverstrips. The corners on the final coverstrips will need to be appliquéd over the ones applied first so that there are no raw edges showing. Prepare the sashing strips and appliqué in place, and bind to complete the quilt.

The No-Marking Method
Transfer a pattern without marking the fabric

Measure quilt and cut a piece of Golden Threads Quilting Paper™ *that measures the exact length to be quilted.*

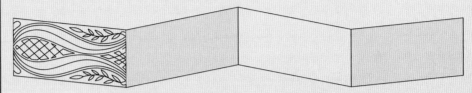

Fold paper accordion style into sections. These should equal the size of one complete repeat of the pattern. Adjust the pattern as needed to fill the whole section, and trace onto the top layer of the folded paper.

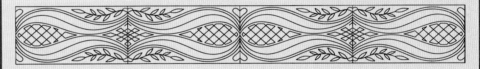

Needlepunch through the folded stack on the sewing machine using a large unthreaded needle. Unfold to reveal the complete design that fits the area to be quilted exactly.

Pin, tape or spray baste in place. Stitch through the paper following the design and tear away after quilting. Pulling your project on the bias causes the paper to pop away from the stitches.

To reuse marked patterns, secure in place with bumpy side up and gently rub the Ultimate Pounce Pad™ *over holes. The chalk will travel through the holes marking the stitching path on your project. The Ultimate Chalk does not rub away and is removable after quilting with the heat of a steam iron or blow dryer.*

For more information visit www.goldenthreads.com.

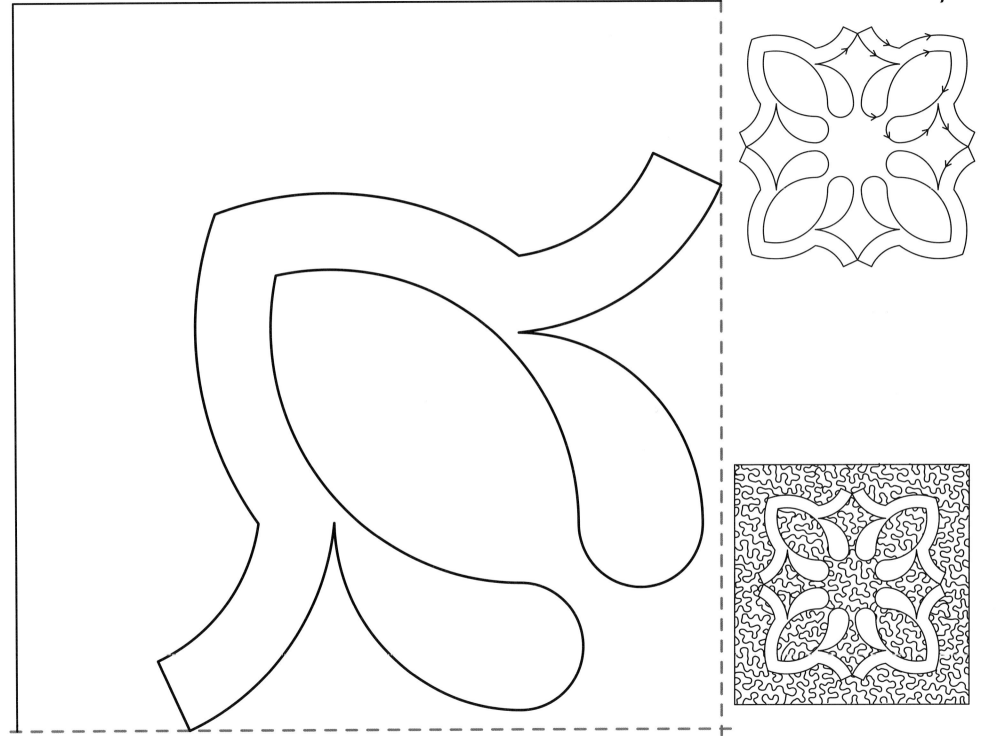

Beautiful Quilts as You Go – *Keryn Emmerson*

Stitch back along the previous line of stitching if possible, or make a small arc as shown on the pattern.

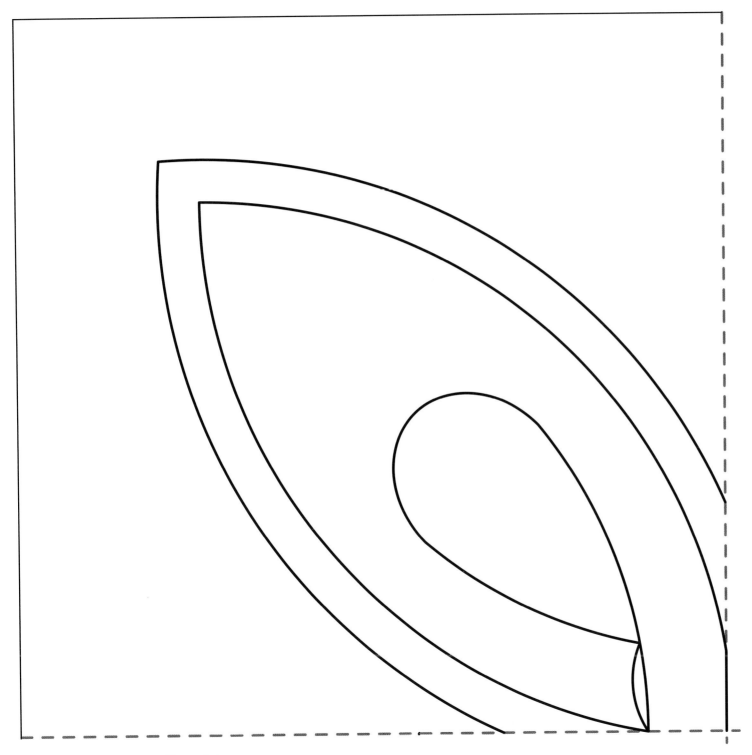

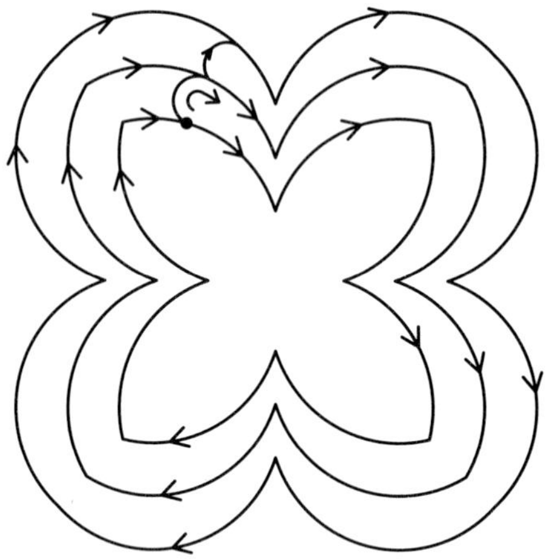

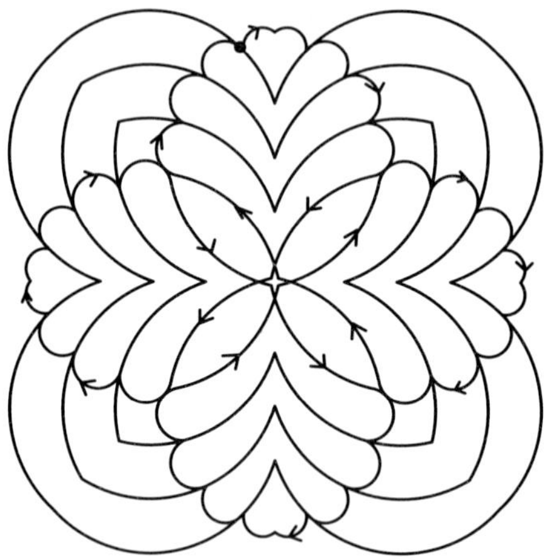

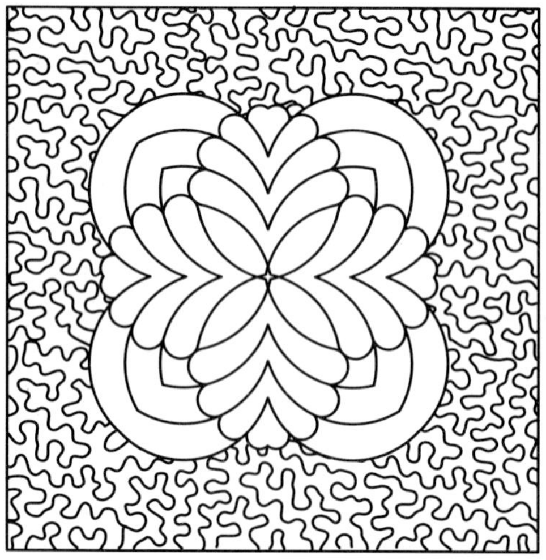

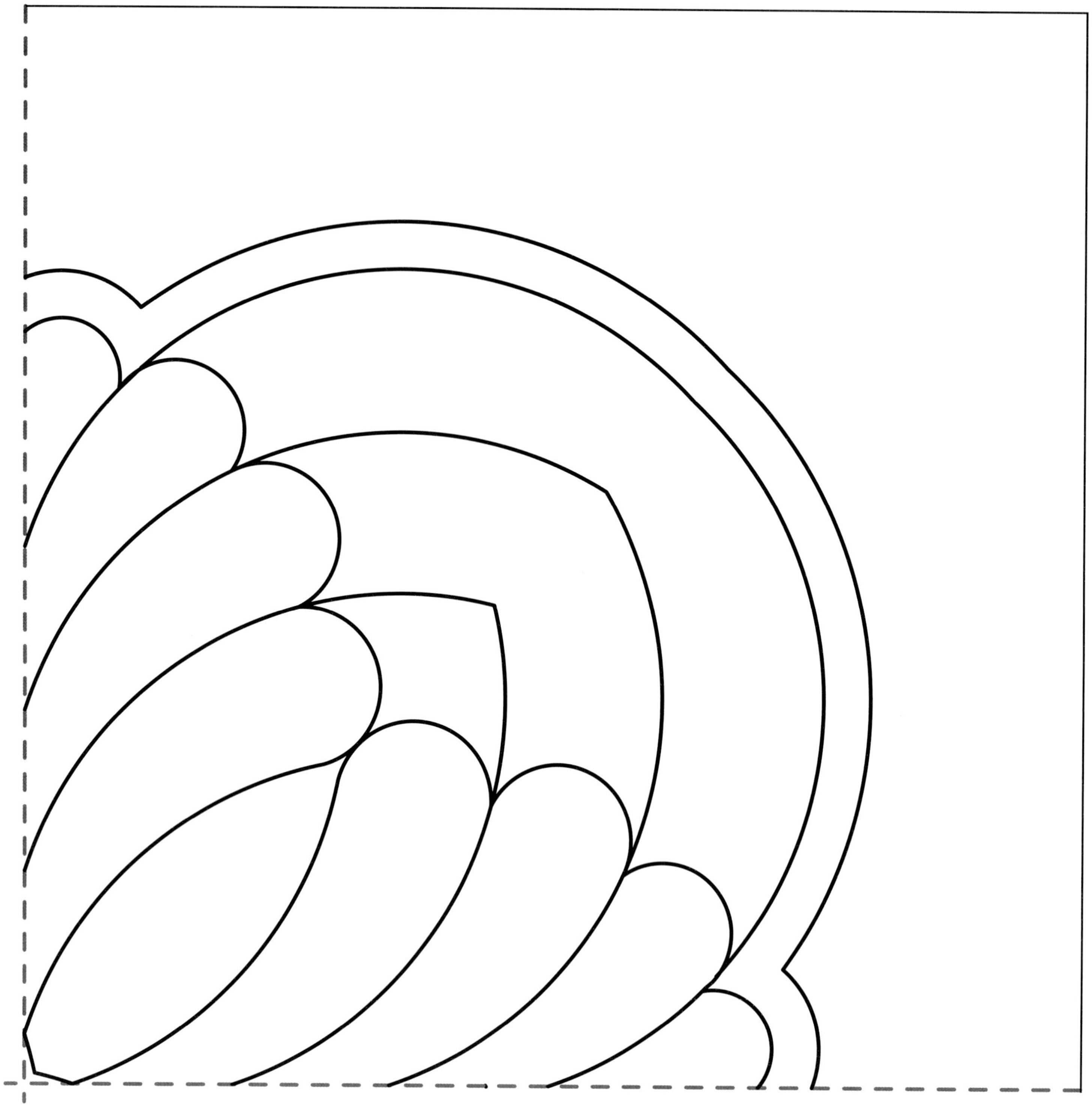

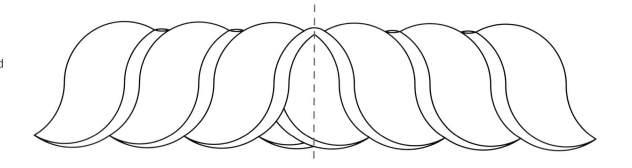

Mark the borders from the corner out, and create a design where the lines overlap in the center of the border.

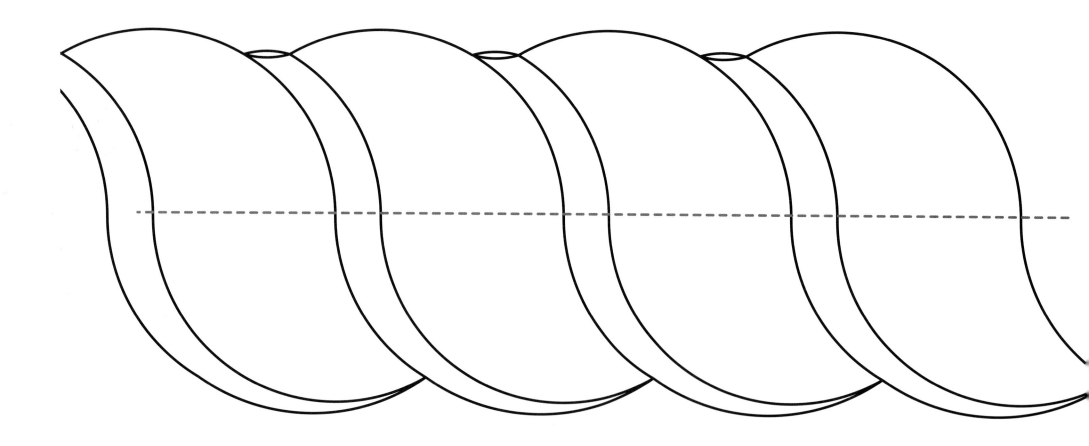

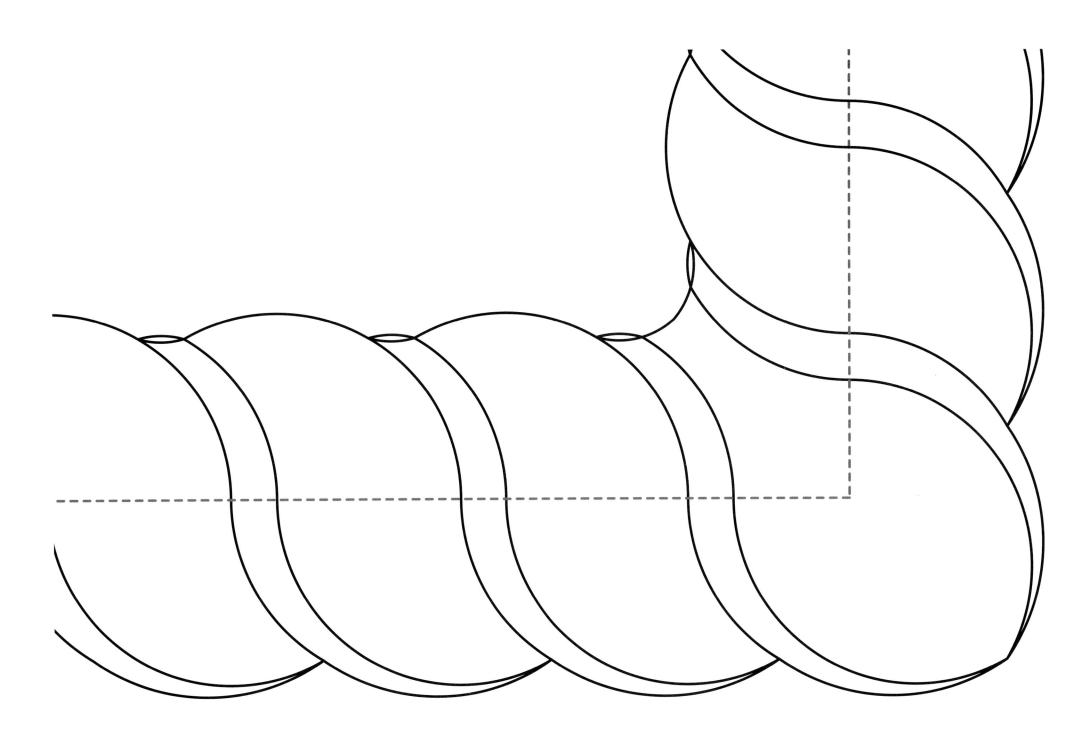

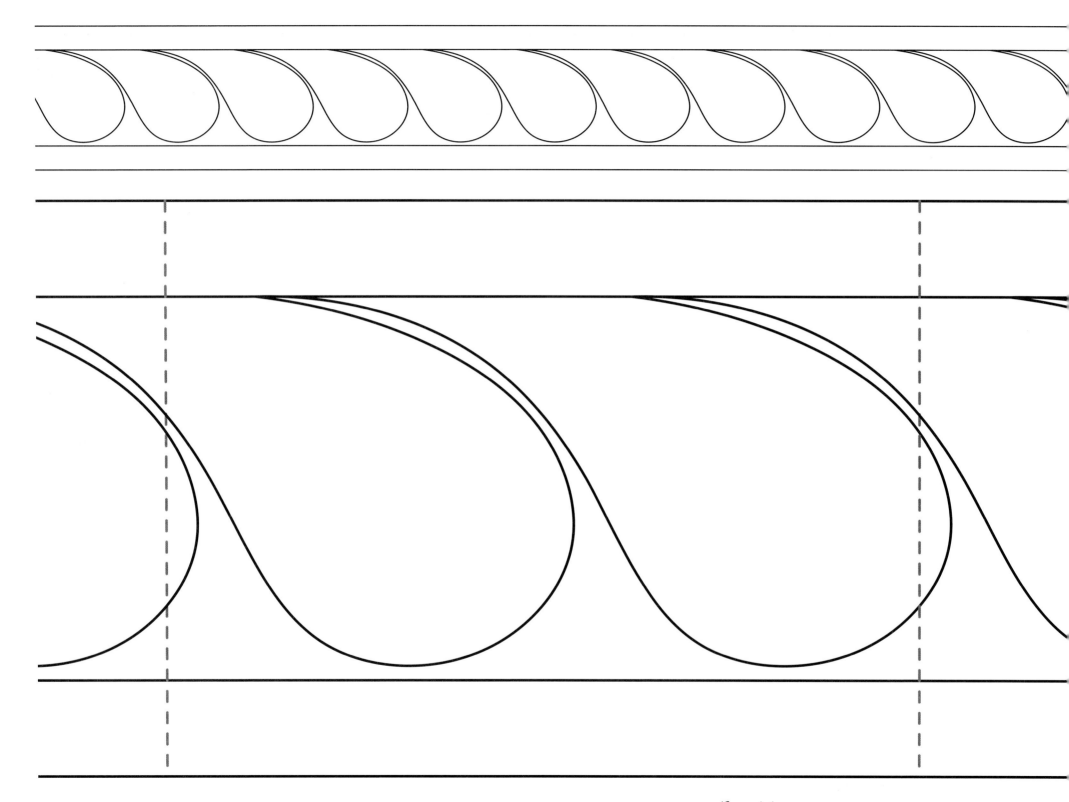

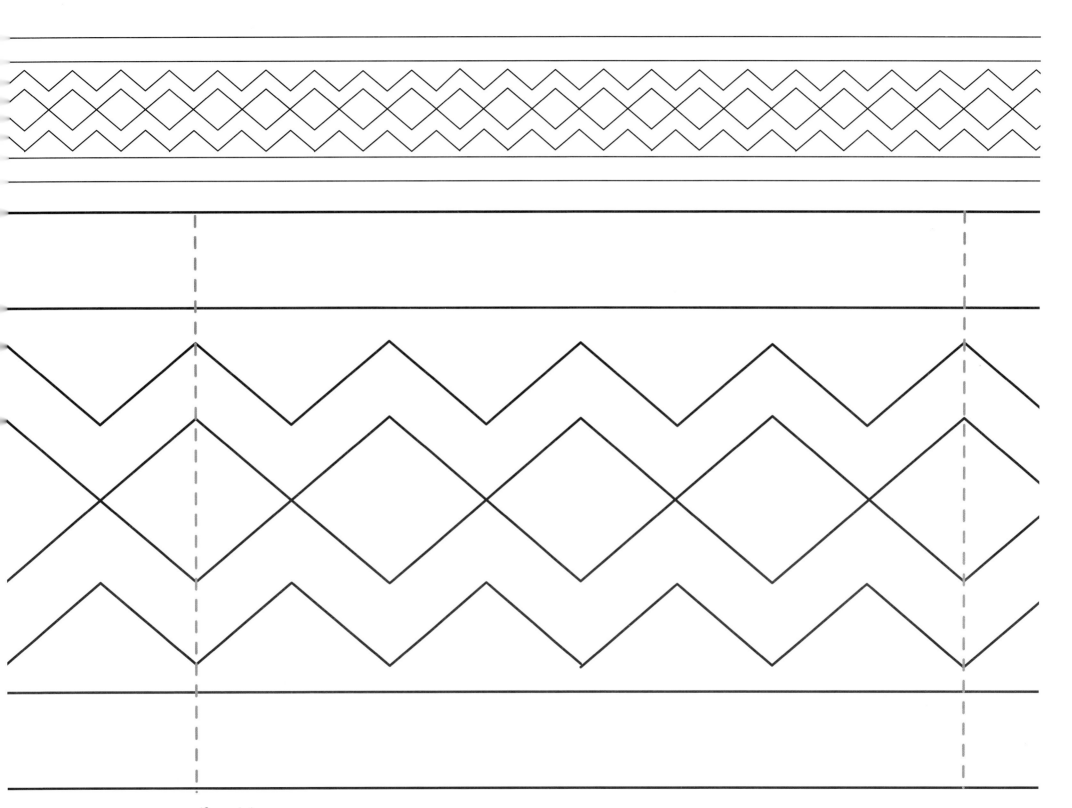

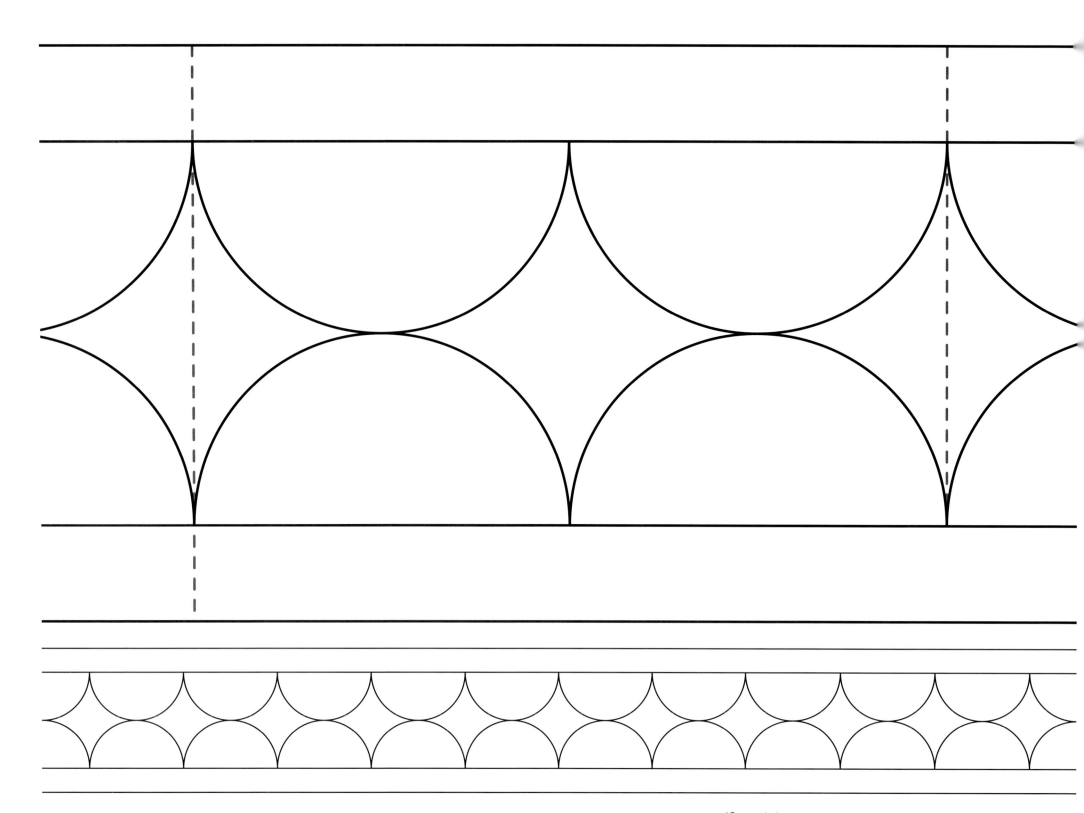

Beautiful Quilts as You Go – *Keryn Emmerson*

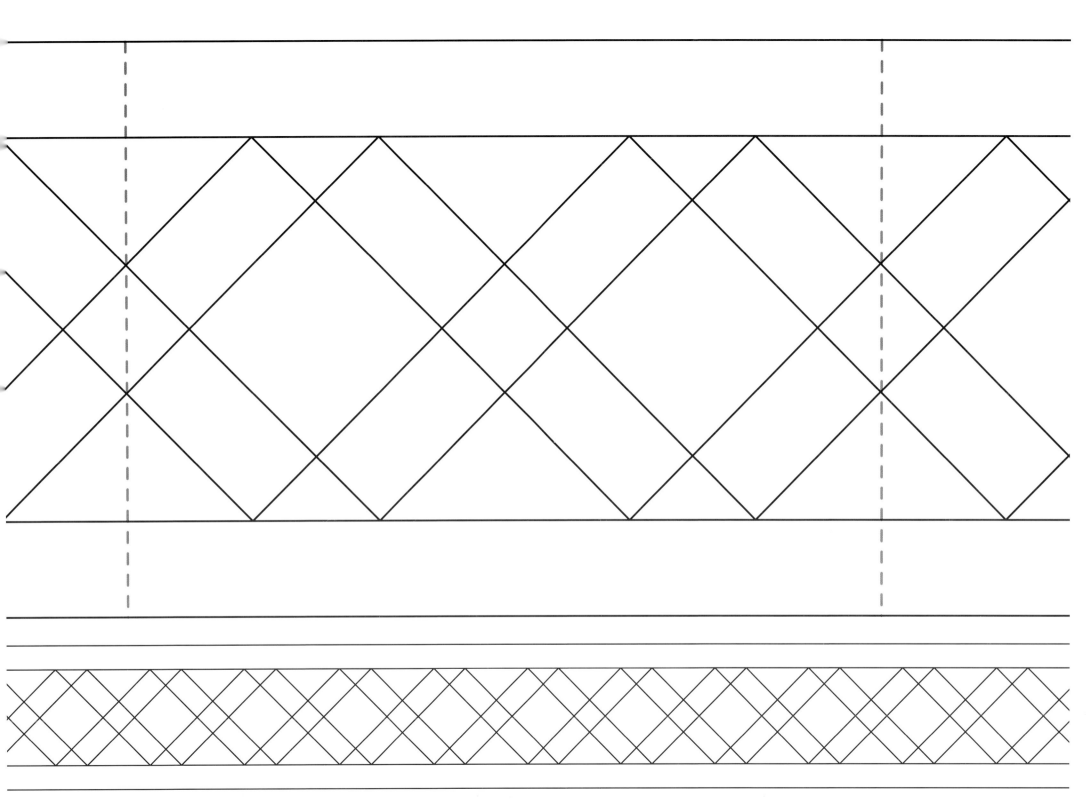

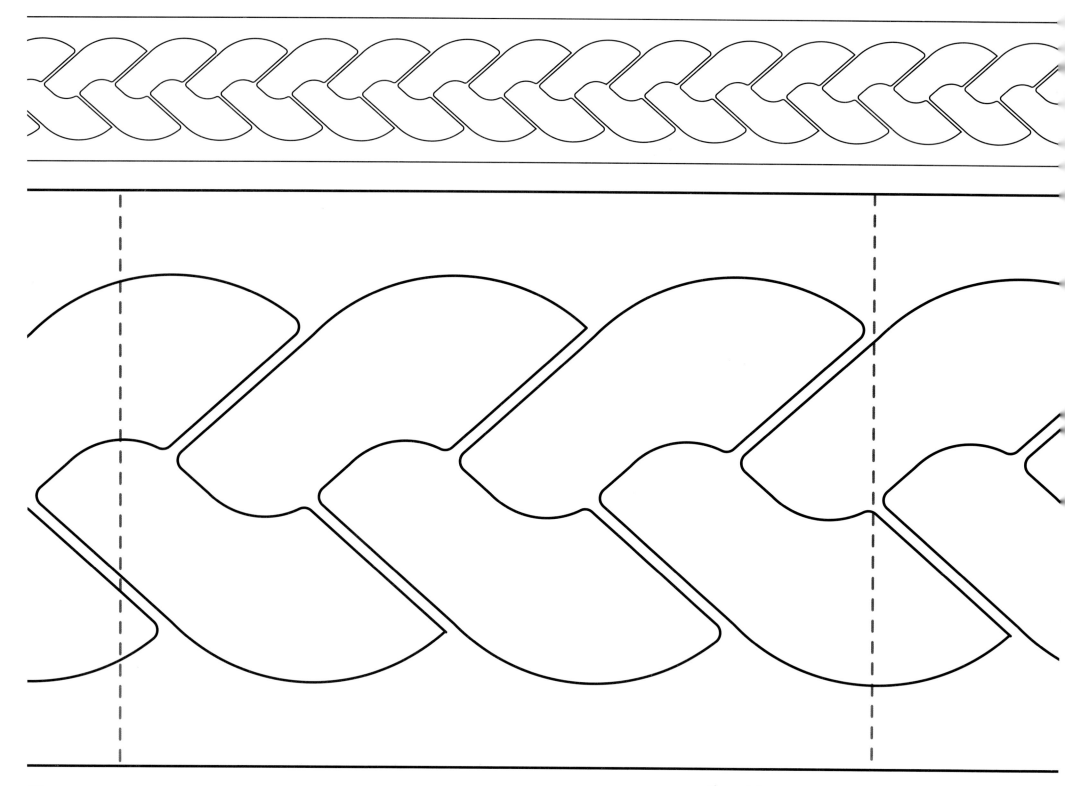

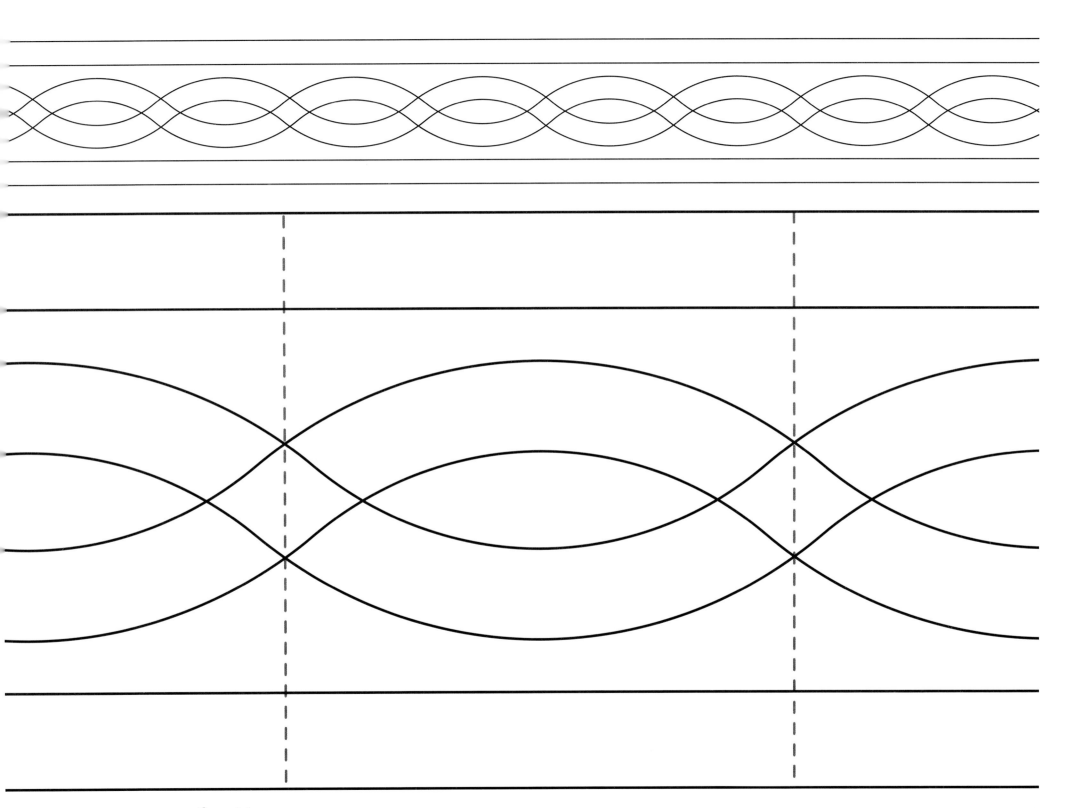

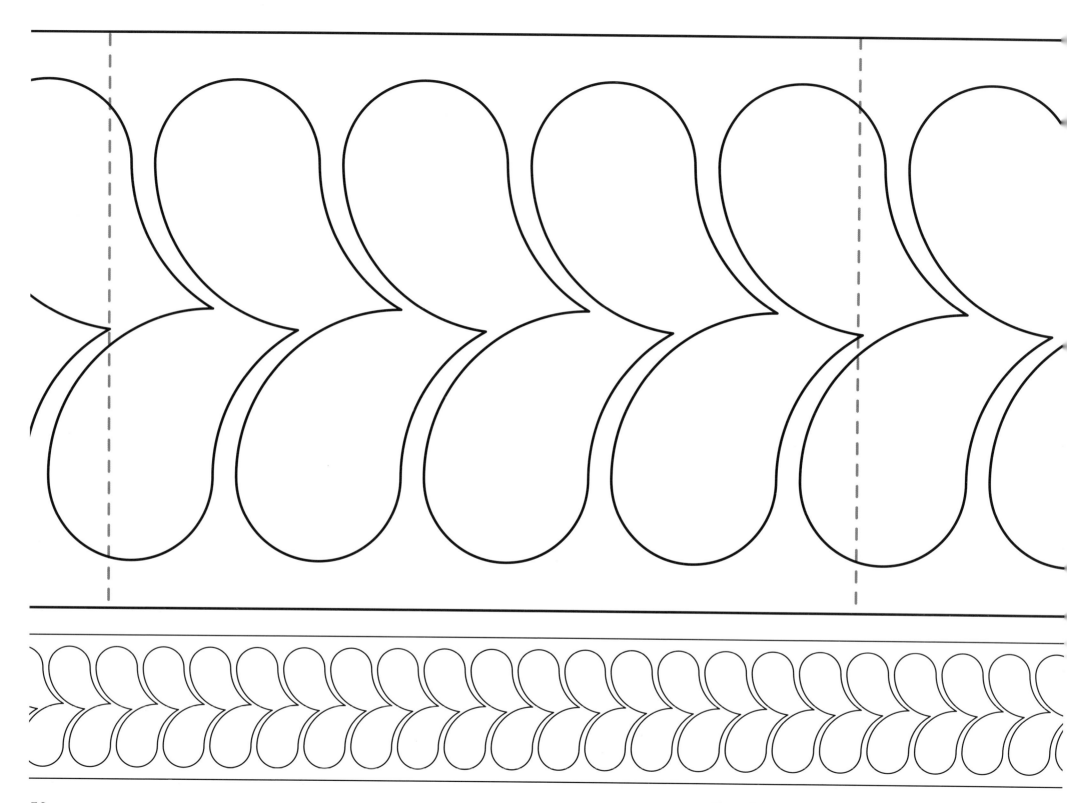

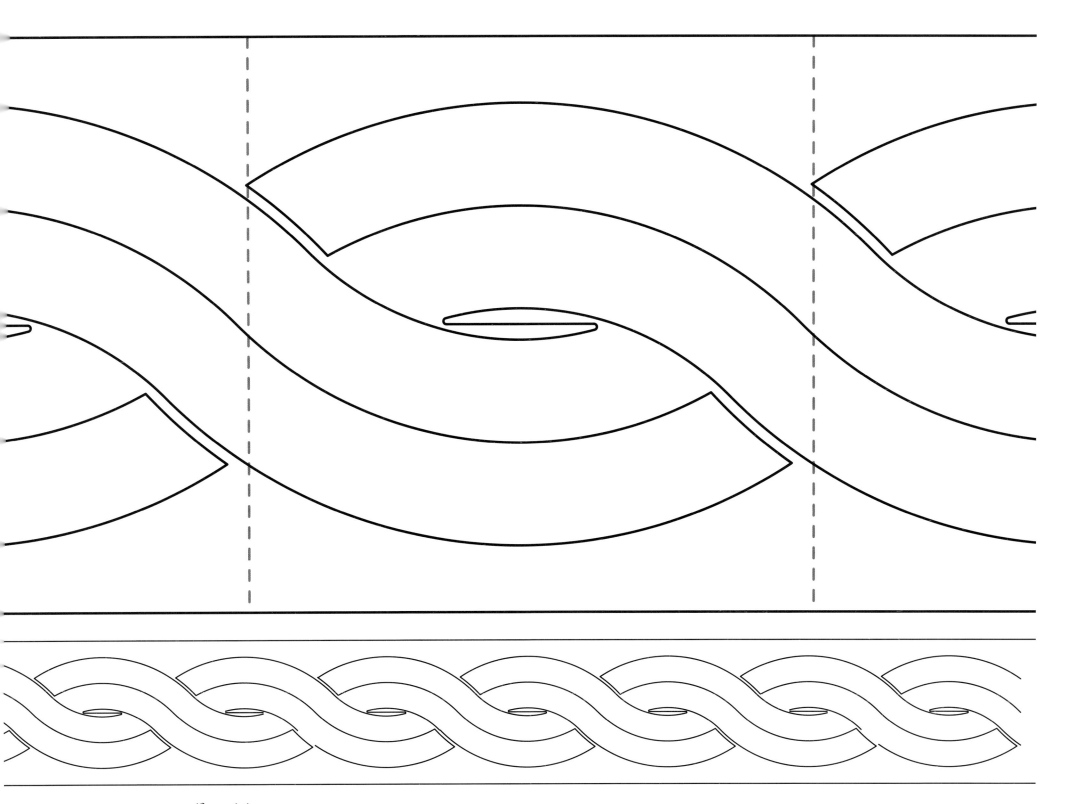

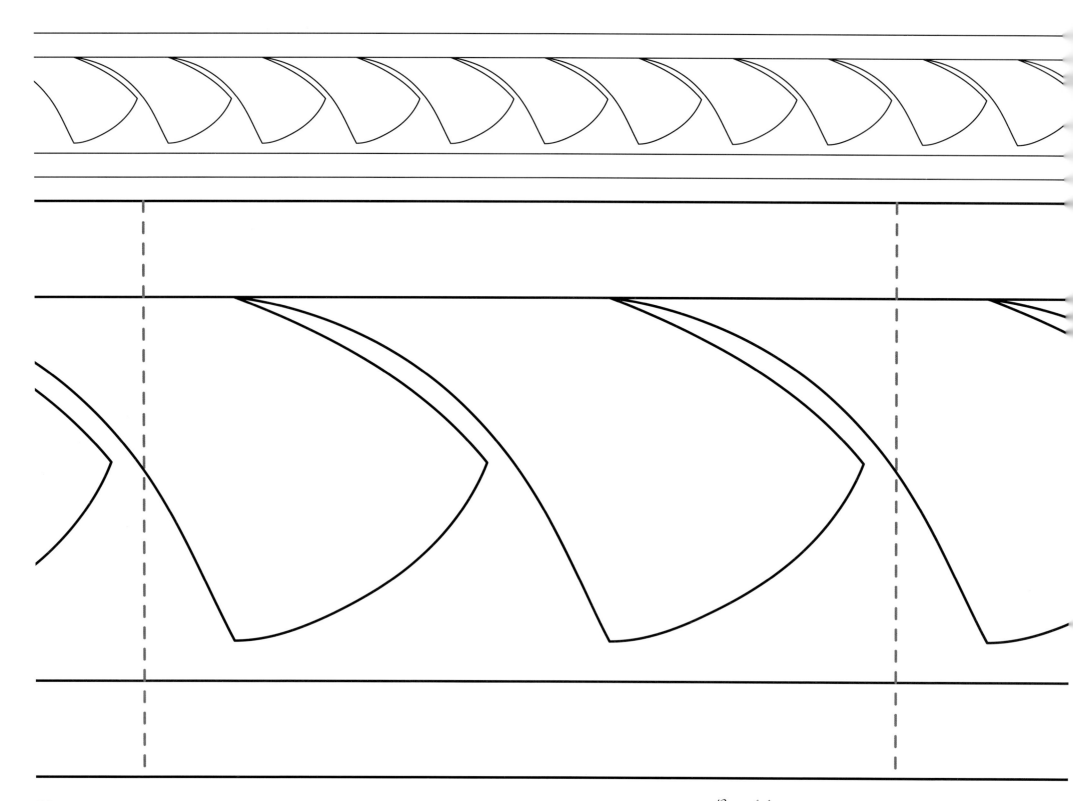

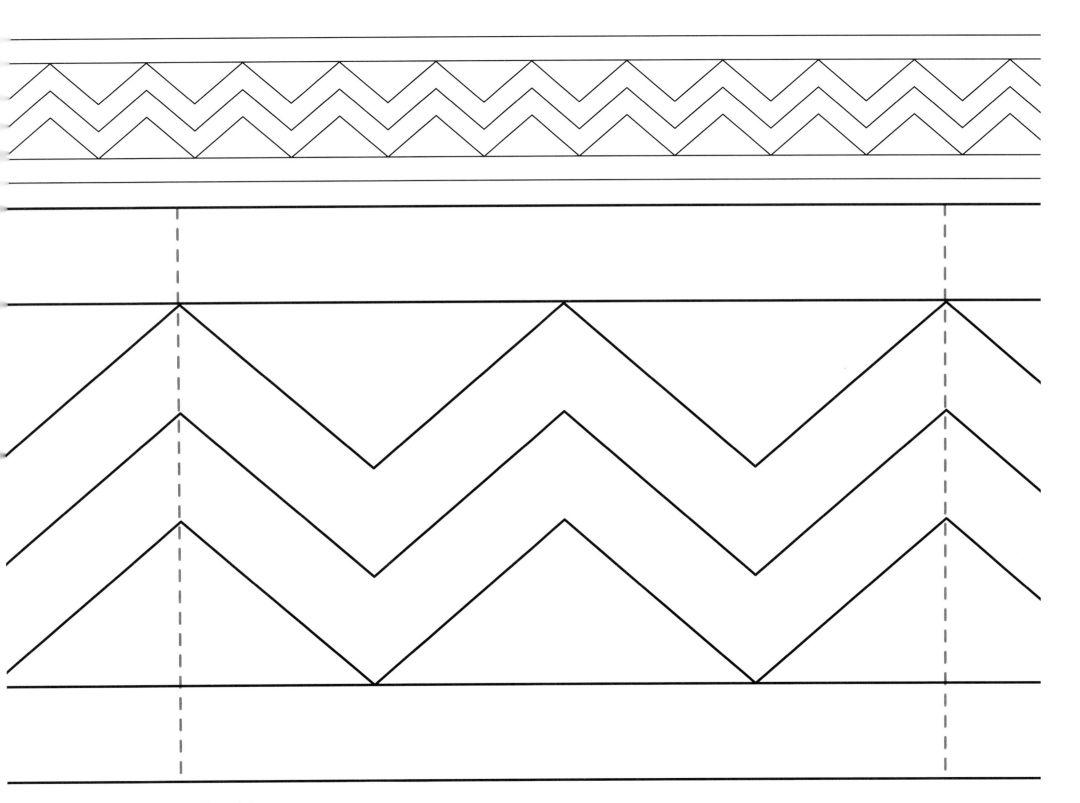

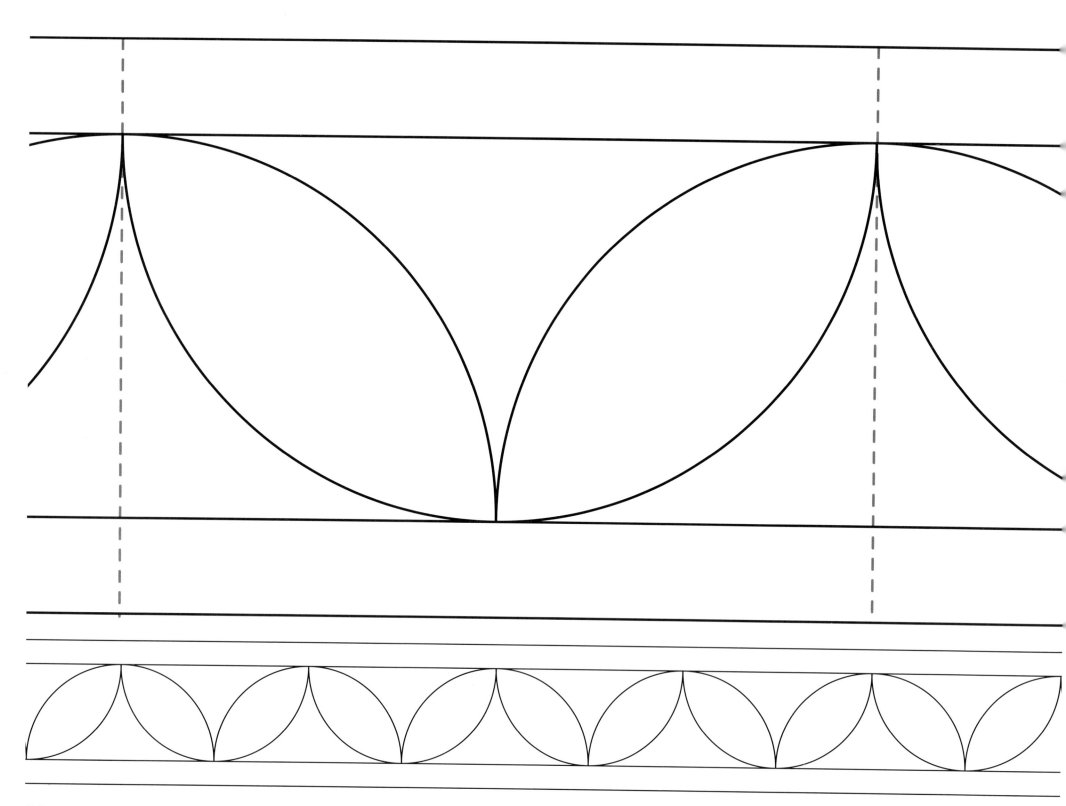

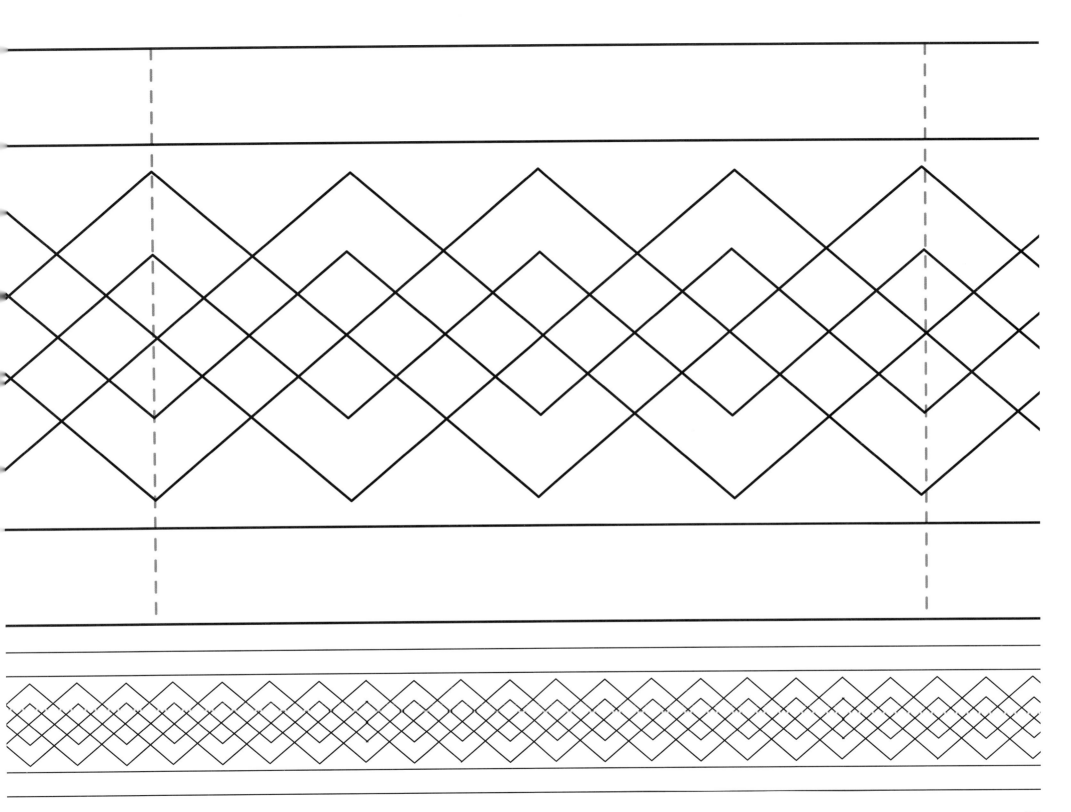

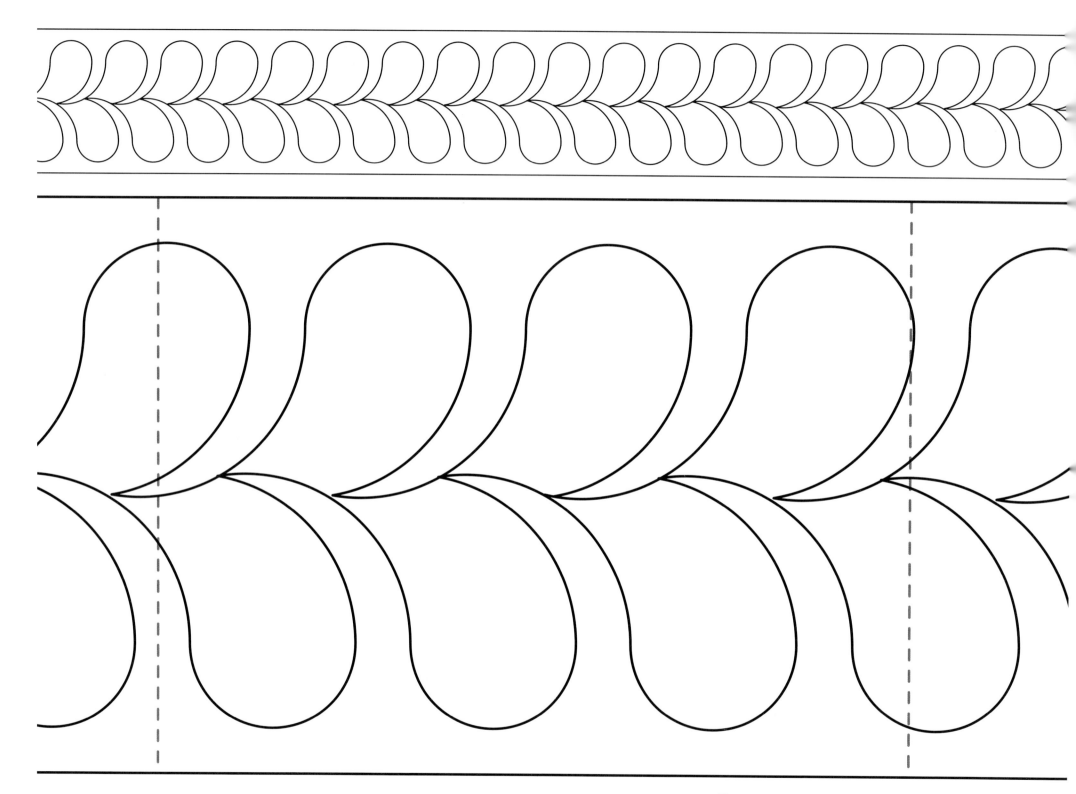

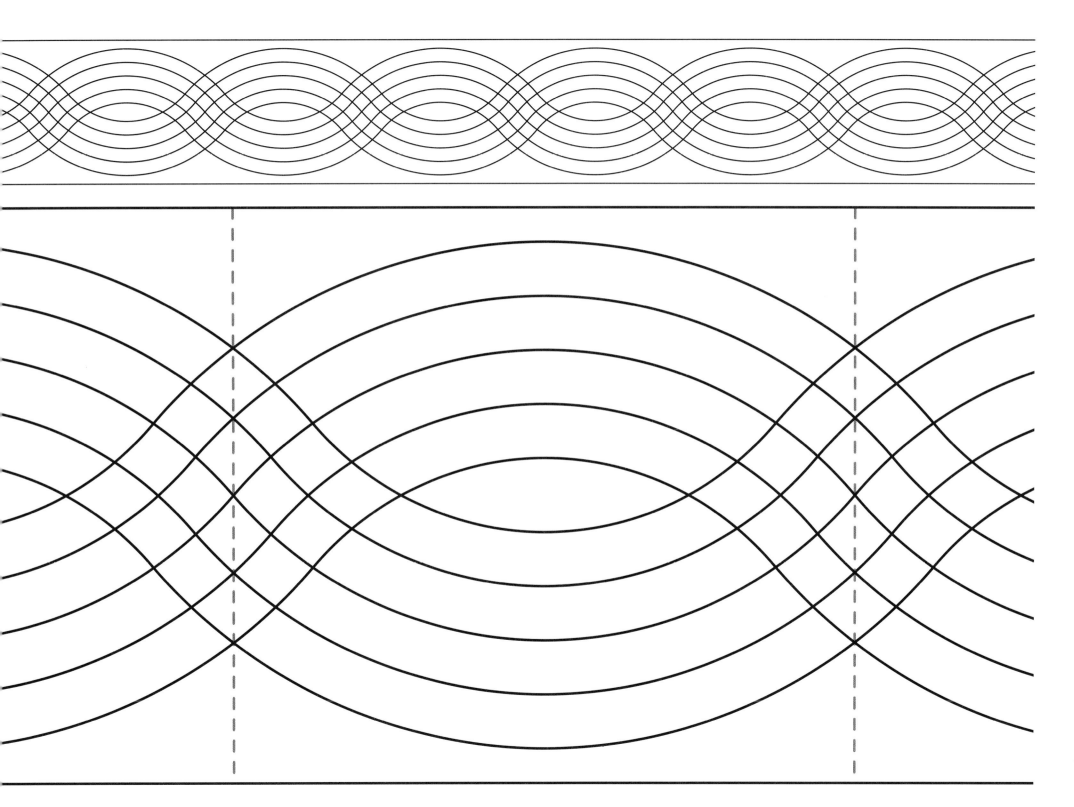

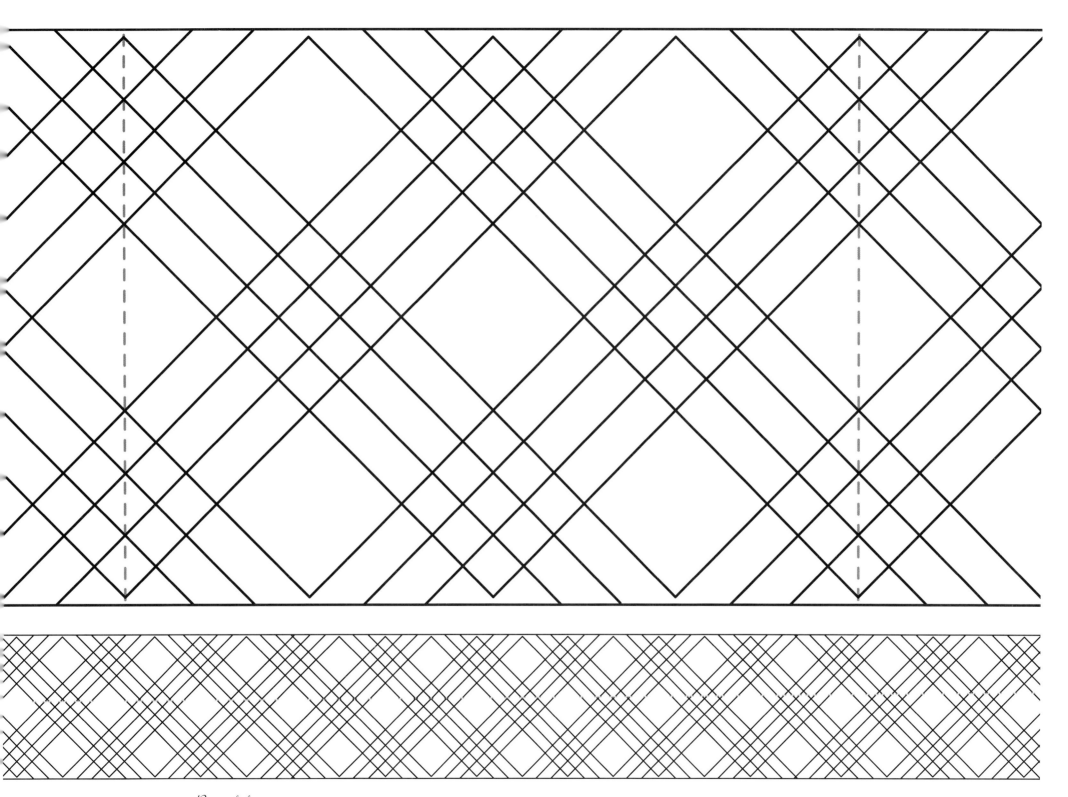

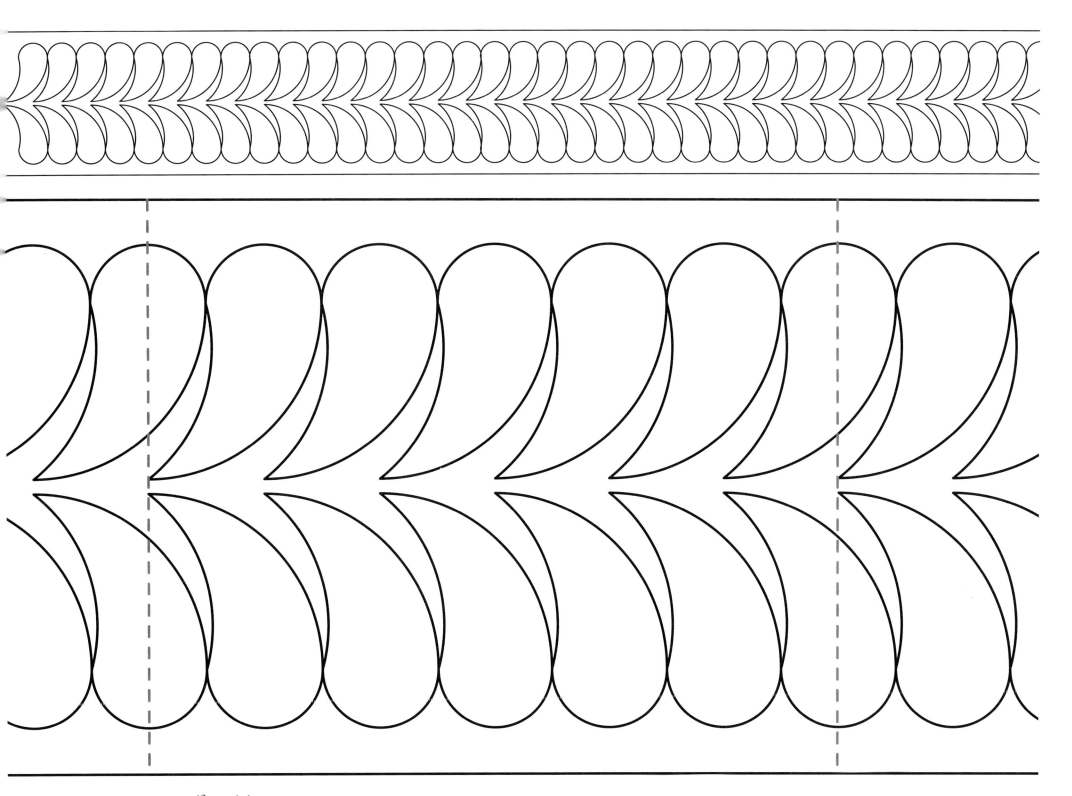

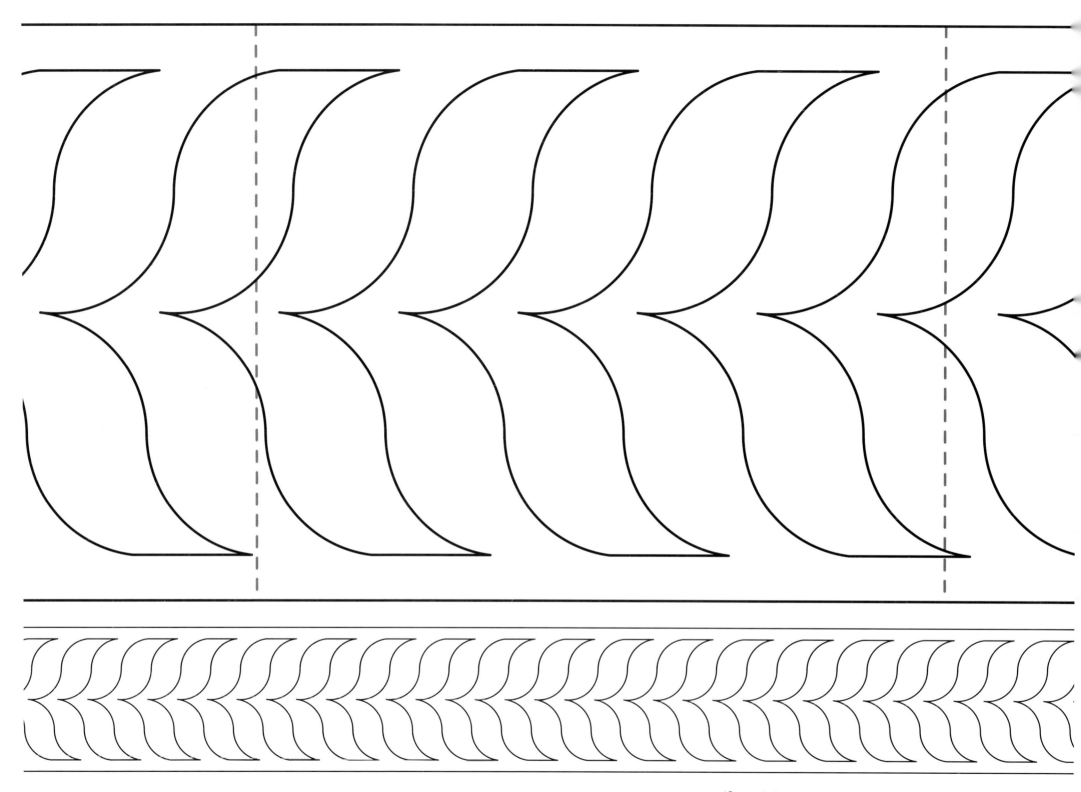

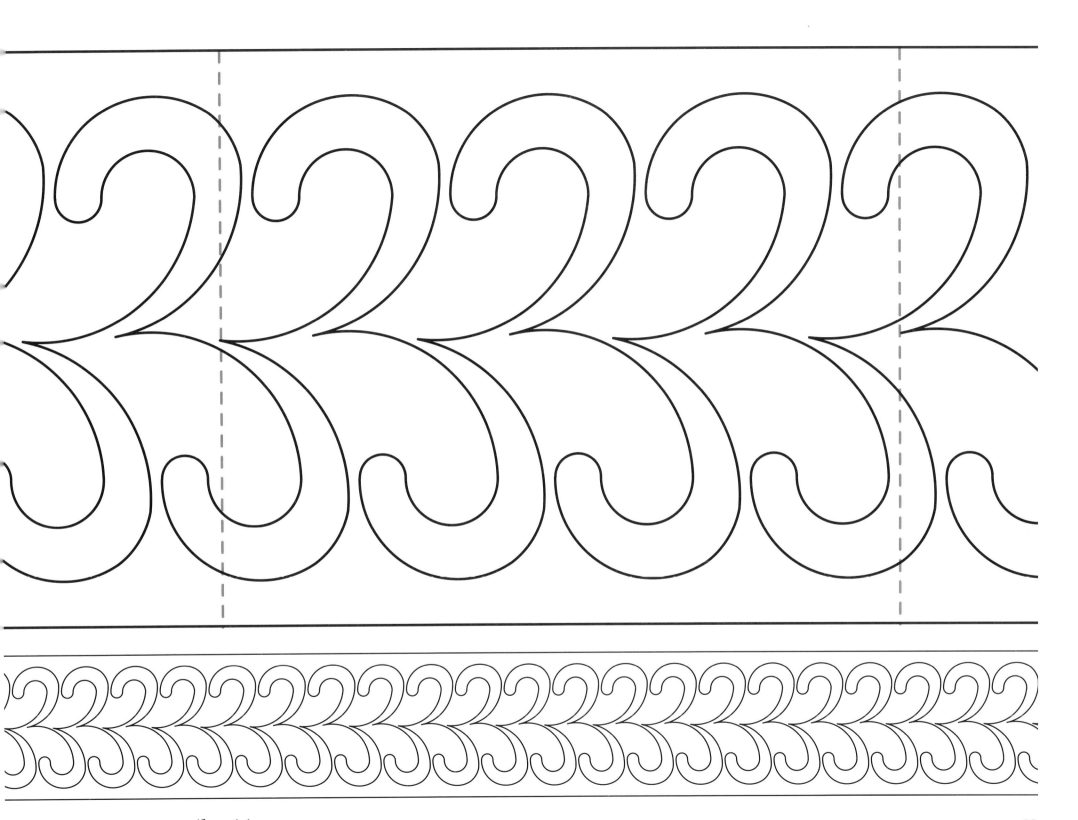

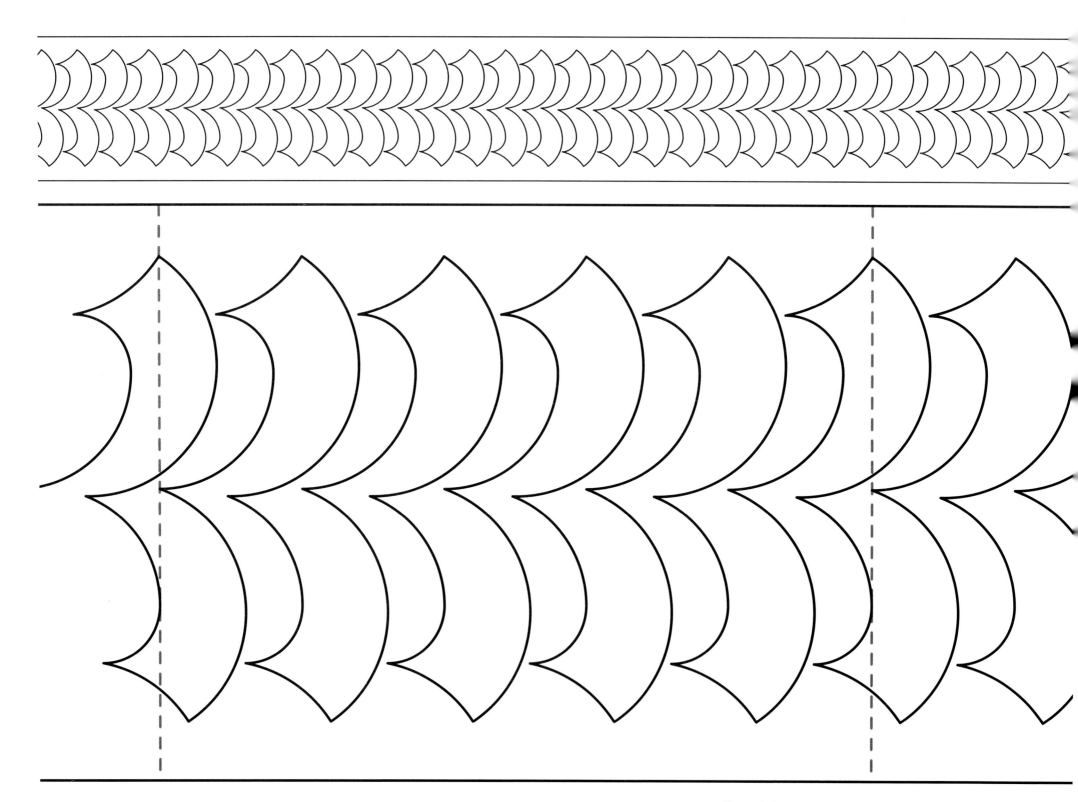

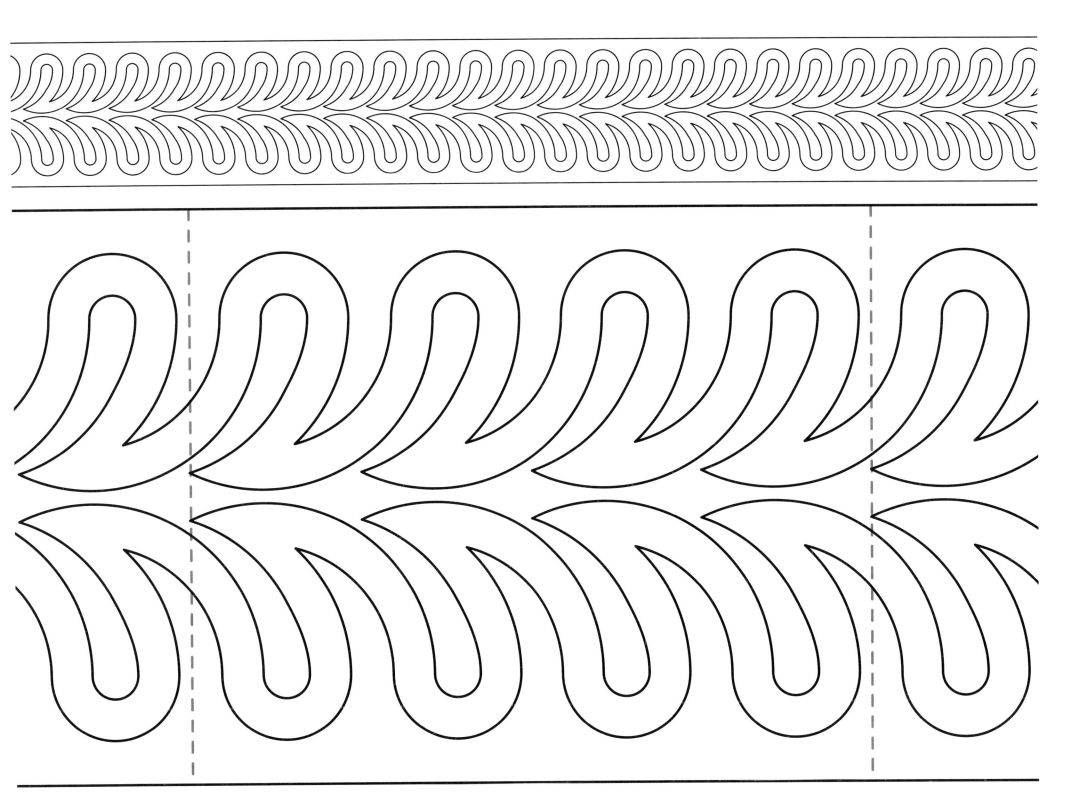

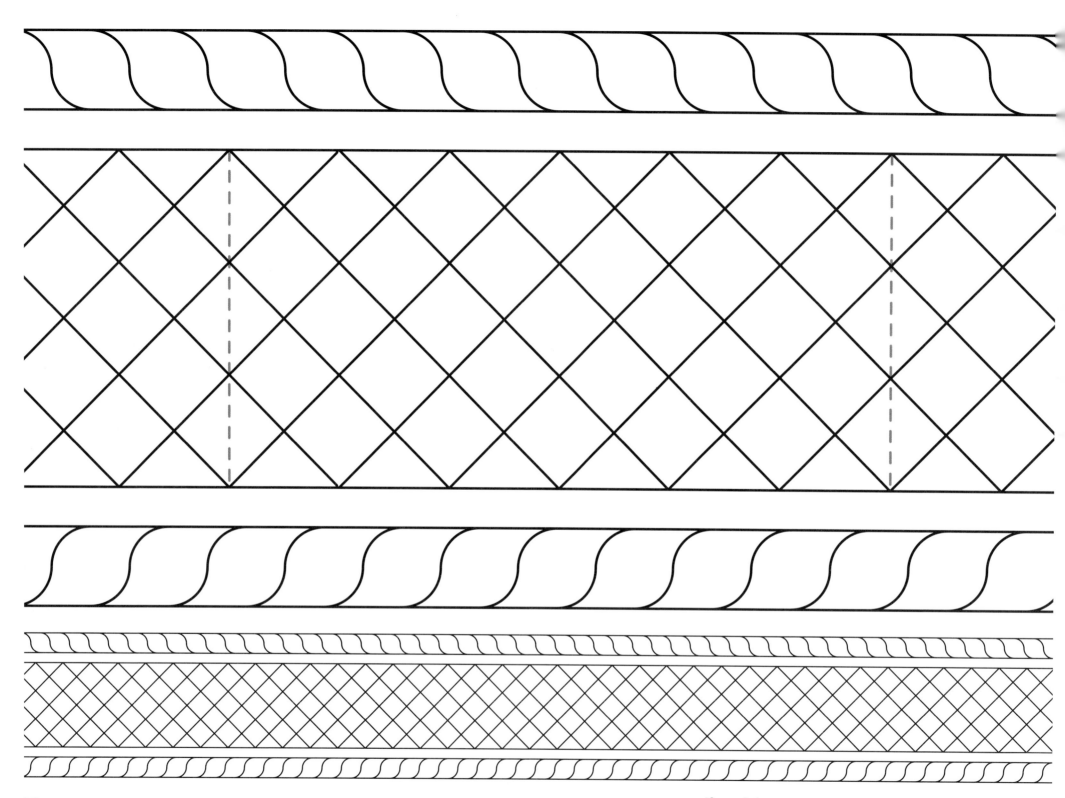

Beautiful Quilts as You Go – *Keryn Emmerson*

78

QAYG Strippy Quilt Projects

Strippy Quilts

Strippy quilts are a traditional form of quilting commonly made in England and Wales, generally for everyday use. They were easily pieced from long strips of material, *usually in two colors* of plain fabric, but print or striped fabric was used as well. Fabrics were most commonly cotton, but wool, flannels, or cotton sateen were also used. In some cases, alternating strips were of patchwork in one or more designs.

They were a showcase of quilting patterns, from the very simple to the very elaborate. One of the main charms of traditional strippy quilts is that there were no rules to follow; the quilter made her own choices about backing and patterns and strip size and fabric content. Because they were utility quilts, they could be put together any way the quilter fancied. The designs could be any possible combination of straight lines and grids, feathers or plain traditional patterns, and they could be exactly positioned to end nicely at the end of the strip, or just be chopped off wherever they ended. No matter how they were stitched, the end result was a beautiful quilt.

The Americans had their own strippy quilts, most commonly found among the Amish. These were termed Bar quilts and often had one or more borders on all four sides, which British strippies do not have. The borders meant there were corners to plan in the quilting, and so there was more work involved. One of the most common Bar quilts was called Joseph's Coat, and was composed entirely of 2" or 3" wide strips of many different colors. The quilting patterns within these narrow strips were simple and often one design was repeated throughout the quilt. These quilts had a vibrancy and impact that belied their simple construction.

Planning

Strippies usually consist of an *odd number* of strips so that the *same color* will be on the edge of the quilt. Strip sizes can vary from 3" to 9" depending on the desired measurements of the finished quilt. I like to make the outer strips wider so that I can have a larger quilting pattern as a border along the sides.

Decide which QAYG joining method you will use, and write down the seam allowance needed for that method. Measure the bed you are making the quilt for and calculate the number of strips, see below, that will be needed to cover the top of the mattress. This will be an odd number, with single large strips on either side to form the side border. The outer strips can be sized to cover the side of the mattress and as much of the base as you want. This is usually between 11" and 15".

Mattress Size		Finished Size of Strips						
		3"	4"	5"	6"	7"	8"	9"
Queen 60"w	# Strips	21	15	13	11	9	7	7
	Dark/Light	11 & 10	8 & 7	7 & 6	6 & 5	5 & 4	4 & 3	4 & 3
	Total width	63"	60"	65"	66"	63"	56"	56"
Double 50"w	# Strips	19	13	11	9	7	7	5
	Dark/Light	10 & 9	7 & 6	6 & 5	5 & 4	4 & 3	4 & 3	3 & 2
	Total width	57"	52"	55"	54"	49"	56"	45"
Twin 36"w	# Strips	13	9	7	7	5	5	5
	Dark/Light	7 & 6	5 & 4	4 & 3	4 & 3	3 & 2	3 & 2	3 & 2
	Total width	39"	36"	35"	42"	35"	40"	45"

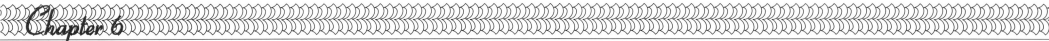

The length of the strips will be the length of the mattress plus the depth at the foot of the bed that needs to be covered. This means that the quilt will cover the whole mattress. If you only want the quilt to come up to the pillow area, start your measurement below the pillows. If you know which pattern you want to use for the borders, you can calculate the length to allow for full repeats of the pattern. The length will be approximately 80" for queen-sized beds. Before cutting the strips, remember to add the appropriate seam allowance depending on the method chosen to join the strips.

Materials

Choose the fabrics for your strips matching the tone and color of the backing fabric to the top fabric. You can choose as few as two fabrics, or have every strip a different fabric.

To calculate how many strips you can cut from the width of the fabric you have chosen, see below. The useable width of fabric after washing and discarding selvages is usually 40". Remember to include the seam allowance in the strip size.

Width of Strips	4"	5"	6"	7"	8"	9"	10"	11"
No. of Strips from 40" Fabric	10	8	6	5	5	4	4	3

If you cannot get all the strips out of one length of fabric, you will need to double that measurement to find the yardage you need to buy.

For most large two-color quilts, double the length of the strip needed to find the yardage of each color required. For more than two colors, you may only need one length. You will need the same amount of fabric for the backing strips as for the front.

If I am buying fabric that could possibly be used for a strippy quilt one day, I buy five yards. If there is a chance I will bind the quilt with that fabric, I buy another yard. Luckily, most strippy quilts can be made of plain fabric that does not cost too much. The backings can be made of several fabrics so that less yardage of each can be purchased, or you can use fabric from your stash. Try to be flexible in your planning if cost is an issue.

Cutting

Wash and press the fabrics for the top and backing. Cut strips the desired size from top and backing fabrics and the batting. Make sure each strip measures the same in length. For the binding, cut enough 2½" strips to equal the perimeter measurement of the finished quilt plus 20".

Marking

Follow the directions in Chapter 2, Marking Tips, on pages 10–12 to mark the chosen designs on your strips. If you always start the pattern at the same end, no matter how long the strip is, the patterns will all end at the same place—that will make the quilt look more balanced. Layer the strips as directed on pages 12–13.

Quilting

Begin with the walking foot work, stabilizing each strip. Fill in the other lines gradually. If you're feeling tired, work on the easy lines and quilt the complex ones when you feel fighting fit. Remember to change thread colors when sewing the contrasting strips. When all the quilting is finished, bind the quilt. Use the color binding of your choice.

Flat Fold Seam Method
Red and White Quilt

Strippy Project Instructions

Requirements

2¼ yards red fabric

2¼ yards backing fabric to match

4½ yards white fabric

4½ yards backing fabric to match

100 yards of thread to match red fabric

1000 yards of thread to match white fabric

3 yards 96" wide batting

Cutting

Wash and iron the fabric. Cut four red strips 9¼" wide and the length of the fabric. Trim ends square and make all strips the same length.

Cut three white strips 9¼" wide and the same length as the red strips.

Cut two white strips 14" wide and the same length as the red strips.

Cut five strips 2½" wide from the remainder of the white fabric for the binding.

Strip Construction

On the *wrong side* of the top red strips, draw a line ½" in from both long sides. This will act as a guide when sewing

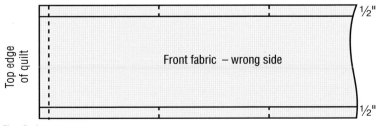

Fig. 6–1

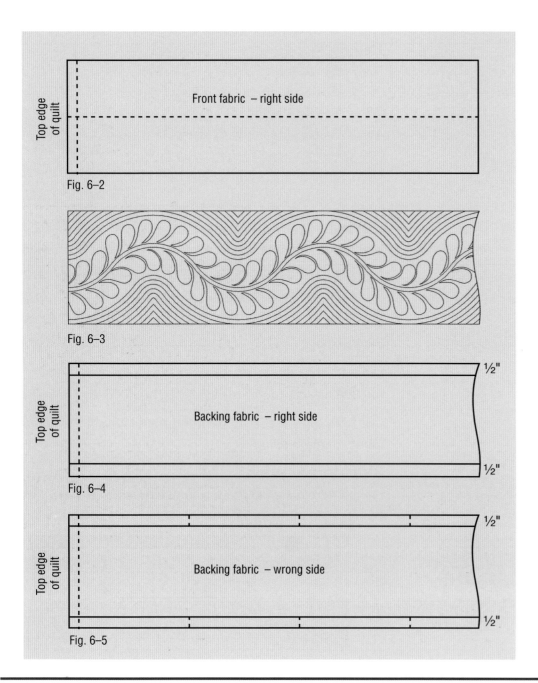

Fig. 6–2

Fig. 6–3

Fig. 6–4

Fig. 6–5

the quilted strips together (fig. 6–1). Draw a line at the start of the strip at right angles to the long sides. From this line, make marks at 10" intervals along both long sides. These marks will act as registration points when assembling the strips.

On the *right side* of the same strips, mark the starting line and the center-line (fig. 6–2). Draw quilting lines 1" in from the long sides, leaving a 7½" design space to fill. Use these markings to position and draw in the design you have chosen (fig. 6–3).

It is necessary to size the designs to fill the space between the outer quilting lines. Either resize the given designs using a copier, or combine simple and ornate designs. *The 6" designs can be enlarged by 120% to make them fit the strips for this project.* Full-size designs are available from Golden Threads (see page 96).

On the *right side* of the darker backing strips, draw a line ½" in from both long sides. This will be the guide for turning under the seam allowance on the back (fig. 6–4).

On the *wrong side*, draw a line at the start of the strip at right angles to the long sides. From this line, make marks at 10" intervals along both long sides (fig. 6–5).

On the lighter strips of the top, draw the designs you have chosen. On the wrong sides of the strips, draw a line at the start of the strip at right angles to the long sides. From this line, make marks at 10" intervals along both sides.

On the wrong sides of the lighter backing strips, draw a line at the start of the strip at right angles to the long sides. From this line, make marks at 10" intervals along both long sides. Layer the strips and quilt.

With the walking foot, quilt stabilizing lines in each strip beginning with the framing lines at each side, then the centerlines of cables, crosshatching, and wave patterns.

After the strips have been stabilized, complete the walking-foot work, then quilt the free-motion parts of the patterns.

On the red strips, take the batting out of the edges on both long sides. Pin the free edge of the red backing strip to the body of the strip, so that it is not caught in the joining seam.

Pin a red strip to a 9¼" white strip, right sides together, matching starting line and 10" registration marks.

Seam together with the walking foot, following the ½" line on the wrong side of the red strip as a guide.

Sew the raw edges together with a line of tacking stitches ⅛" away from the edges. Trim the seam to a fraction under ½".

Press under the free edge of the red backing strip, using the ½" line on the right side as a guide. Lay the quilt on a flat surface and pin the folded edge of the backing to the stitching of the seam, covering all the raw edges. Place the pins vertically to make hand sewing the edge easier.

Slip stitch the folded edge to the fabric by the joining seam, taking care to keep the seam flat and tight.

Alternate the red and white center strips, then add the wide white borders and bind. Congrats! Hang. Enjoy!

Cables

Waves

Crosshatching

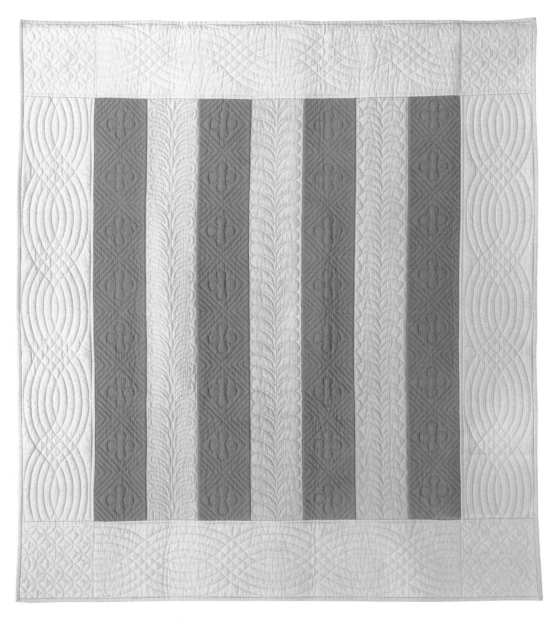

Seam and Bind Method
Strippy Quilt with Corner Blocks

Strippy Quilt Construction

Seam and Bind Method

I used only two colors because it was made for a specific area that needed a quiet quilt, but you can make yours using Amish-style colors with every strip different. Remember that quilting does not show up as well on dark or print fabrics, so restrict your choices to pale and medium colors or bright colors that are not too dark.

The cutting is slightly different in this quilt because the strips are cut across the width of the fabric and folded in half so that the front of the strip is the same as the back. If you want to use different material on the front and back, just cut the strips 6½" wide. The final measurements of the quilt will depend on the width of your fabric because the strips are cut crosswise.

Requirements

- 1¾ yard medium solid fabric for a two-color quilt
- 4⅜ yards light solid fabric, including borders and binding
- 4⅜ yards of 150 cm batting. If batting is wider, then reduce length accordingly. Avoid anything that's extra thick or has a lot of loose fibers. Both will affect the ease of stitching.
- Cotton thread to match both fabrics

Cutting

The strips are cut 13" wide and folded in half, lengthwise. This creates the front and back of the strip and helps stabilize the strip because you have only two raw edges instead of four. You will cut the border strips according to the measurements of your quilt.

Cut four 13" strips from the full width of the medium fabric, and three from the light fabric.

Cut six 1¼" strips from the light-colored fabric to bind the seams.

Cut six 2½" strips from the light-colored fabric for binding the finished quilt.

Cut seven 6½" strips from the full width of the batting.

Preparation

Fold each 13" strip in half lengthwise and press thoroughly. The center crease will help you construct the sandwich of material and batting. Transfer the quilting designs to the fabric strip. Trace the geometric pattern of your choice onto the right half of the medium strips.

Draw a line down the center of the right half of the strip using a quilting ruler; it will be 3¼" in from the edge (fig. 6–6). Align the centerline of the design with the centerline of the strip for the greatest accuracy (fig. 6–7). If you are using the same geometric pattern on all the medium strips, make sure you mark each strip with the pattern beginning at the same place so they will be aligned across the quilt (fig. 6–8).

Cut the batting strips to the exact length of the fabric strips, taking care to make the cuts at a ninety-degree angle to any folds in the batting. Sandwich the batting and the marked strip.

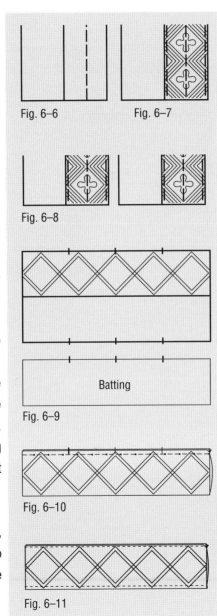

Fig. 6–6   Fig. 6–7

Fig. 6–8

Batting

Fig. 6–9

Fig. 6–10

Fig. 6–11

Strip Construction

At this and every stage of construction, mark the quarter and halfway points of the pieces to be joined, including the batting, and match them when pinning together (fig. 6–9). This ensures that everything is in exactly the right place, no matter how buckled the strips look.

Keeping all the raw edges even, pin around the open sides of the strip. Place pins every inch and a half so that nothing will shift when stitched (fig. 6–10). It looks pretty horrible with the pins distorting it, but if the edges are exact, the strip will lie flat after sewing.

The next step is to stabilize the strips by tacking them together on the machine with the walking foot. For tacking purposes, I use normal thread in a light. contrasting color. Dark threads may leave marks when removed, especially if they've been left in the material for any length of time.

Using a walking foot, sew only the long open edge, having the needle centered and using the edge of the walking foot as a guide against the raw edge (fig. 6–11). Stitch length should be 3–3.5 and the thread tension normal.

Unpin the short ends and make sure that the batting reaches right up to the middle crease of the strip. Put your hands inside the strip and push the batting into place. Pin along the crease and sew the same way.

Pin baste the strip every 4". You can use normal pins for this. The geometric patterns have a framework that secures the whole strip. Determine which of these lines you'll be quilting first, and place additional pins where they will not interfere (fig. 6–12).

Quilting the Geometric Designs

Using a walking foot, stitch the major lines carefully. Do not pull or stretch the material; hold the material flat and relaxed and let the walking foot control how much fabric goes through. Stitch slowly and follow the lines exactly. Leave the needle down in the fabric when turning the piece; make sure before you begin stitching again that all the layers are straight and aligned to avoid pleats and puckers. Make sure that the traveling lines between design elements are hidden within the eventual seam allowances.

It helps to quilt the small motifs in the geometrics first; they're tiny and very easy to pull out if you're not satisfied. Stitch the other lines, removing the pins as necessary.

Quilting the Curved Designs

Prepare the light strips in the same way as you did the dark strips. Quilt them with either a walking foot or free-motion quilting. Always bring both threads to the surface and hold them there until you've taken a few stitches; they'll be much easier to tie off and bury beneath the top fabric.

Quilt Construction

After all the strips are finished, lay them out on a table in the correct order. Make sure that all the folded edges are to the same side, either left or right (fig. 6–13). When you sew them together, it's much easier to be sewing an open edge to a folded edge each time; it helps to control the bulk.

Match centers and edges exactly; pin every 1½". You may have to ease the strips together slightly. If one is longer, have that strip on the bottom and the foot will help to ease it in. Set the needle position to the <u>left</u> and sew the strips together using the edge of the foot as a guide.

Bind the seams with the 1¼" strips. Machine quilting causes the strip to contract; when applying the binding, do not stretch the seam because it will be longer than the quilted strip. Measure the length of the strip along the centerline and transfer this mark to the seam-binding strip. Mark the center and quarter marks of the binding strip and pin to the seam, matching

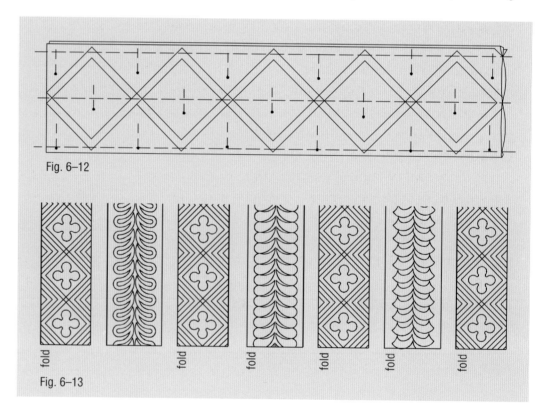

Fig. 6–12

Fig. 6–13

center and quarter marks on the quilt. What you are aiming to do is bring the seam length back in line to the quilted strip (fig. 6–14). All binding strips should finish the same length.

Trim the seam to reduce bulk. Do not trim the material and batting next to the binding, otherwise they'll stick up and make a noticeable ridge. Trim the three layers of the bottom strip and the remaining fabric from the top strip. Fold the binding over to enclose the seam and tack or hem in place. Cut off excess binding.

Side Borders

The side borders of the quilt are cut 18" wide and exactly the same measurement as the binding strips. The batting is 9" wide and the same length. Prepare the same as the other strips; begin marking in the center and move out toward the ends of the strip.

Pin baste the marked strip. Because of the border width, it may also help to have lines of machine basting across the strip and at the quarter and halfway points (fig. 6–15). Quilt with the walking foot. Attach and bind these borders to the main part of the quilt.

Final Borders and Corners

I used a different method to attach the final borders to ensure a smooth, even look. Many quilts are spoiled by rippled borders that will not lie flat, so it's worth taking more care over these final steps. Using this method, the quilt will lie flatter and the seams will be less noticeable.

The length of the final border will be the measurement through the center of the whole quilt (fig. 6–16). Cut the four border strips 9" wide and the final measurement of the whole quilt. Mark the centers and quarters of each strip.

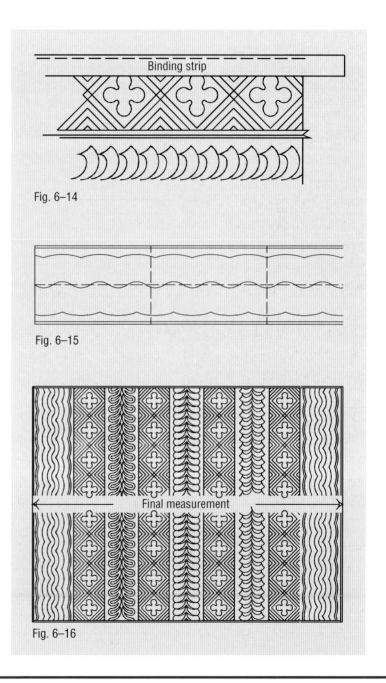

Binding strip

Fig. 6–14

Fig. 6–15

Final measurement

Fig. 6–16

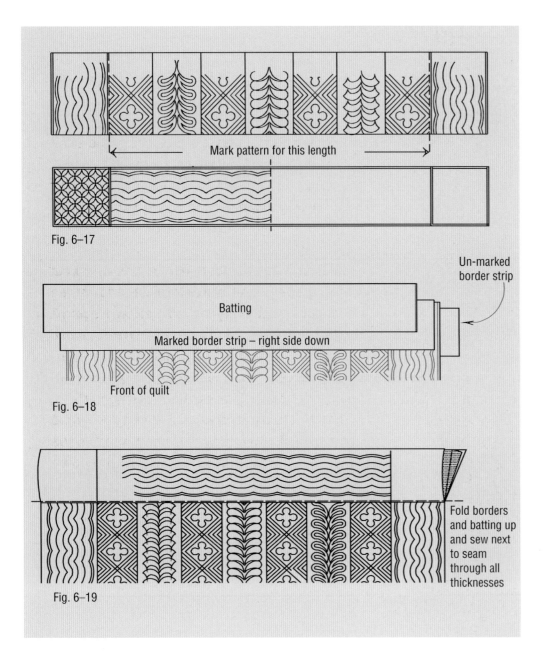

Mark pattern for this length

Fig. 6–17

Batting

Marked border strip – right side down

Front of quilt

Fig. 6–18

Un-marked border strip

Fold borders and batting up and sew next to seam through all thicknesses

Fig. 6–19

Measure the internal striped area of the quilt through the middle (fig. 6–17), and halve this number. Beginning in the center of one border strip, mark the border pattern for this length on both sides of the centerline. You should have an unmarked square at either end of the strip.

With the *right side* of the quilt facing you, pin the unmarked border to the back of the quilt, matching quarters and center. Pin the marked border, face down, to the front, making sure all the edges are exactly even. Be as fussy as you like. Take the batting and pin on top of the marked border piece (fig. 6–18).

When sewing the seam, use something flat like a small ruler to depress the batting in front of the foot. Trim the seam as before, leaving the border batting intact. Lay the quilt out flat and pull the back border out straight, finger pressing the seam from the back. Fold the batting and front border up and flatten the seam as before. Pin ¼" away from the seam taking care not to pull the material crooked. Sew through all layers, having the edge of the presser foot against the seam (fig. 6–19).

Lay the quilt out flat and pin the raw edges together matching centers and quarters exactly. Sew all raw edges together including the short ends. Baste and quilt the border pattern as before, taking more time and care because by now you are maneuvering nearly the whole quilt. Choose the corner pattern design for free-motion quilting.

Add the last border and the quilt is in one piece. Quilt as before. Bind the raw edges and attach a rod pocket. Soak and rinse the finished quilt to remove the marking ink. Dry in the shade, changing the quilt's position regularly to avoid a mark line from the line. Hang the quilt in your chosen spot and admire it. Congratulations!

Bonus Pattern Layout

Border and Corner Fillers

Old Durham and Welsh quilters often used corner-fill patterns to avoid having to turn the pattern around the corner, so I have borrowed their method. It takes extra planning and effort to make the pattern flow uninterrupted around a quilt with two different border lengths, and using this method allows you to resize the quilt without having to agonize over the border.

I would advise you not to get too anxious about making every quilt a masterpiece and refrain from pulling out every incorrect stitch. Regard it instead as a learning piece and leave in those slight imperfections. Hand quilting is not perfectly regular, and machine quilting does not have to be either. If you make a glaring mistake, unpull just those stitches and start again where you left off. Someday you may need those imperfections to convince people that you once could not machine quilt either!

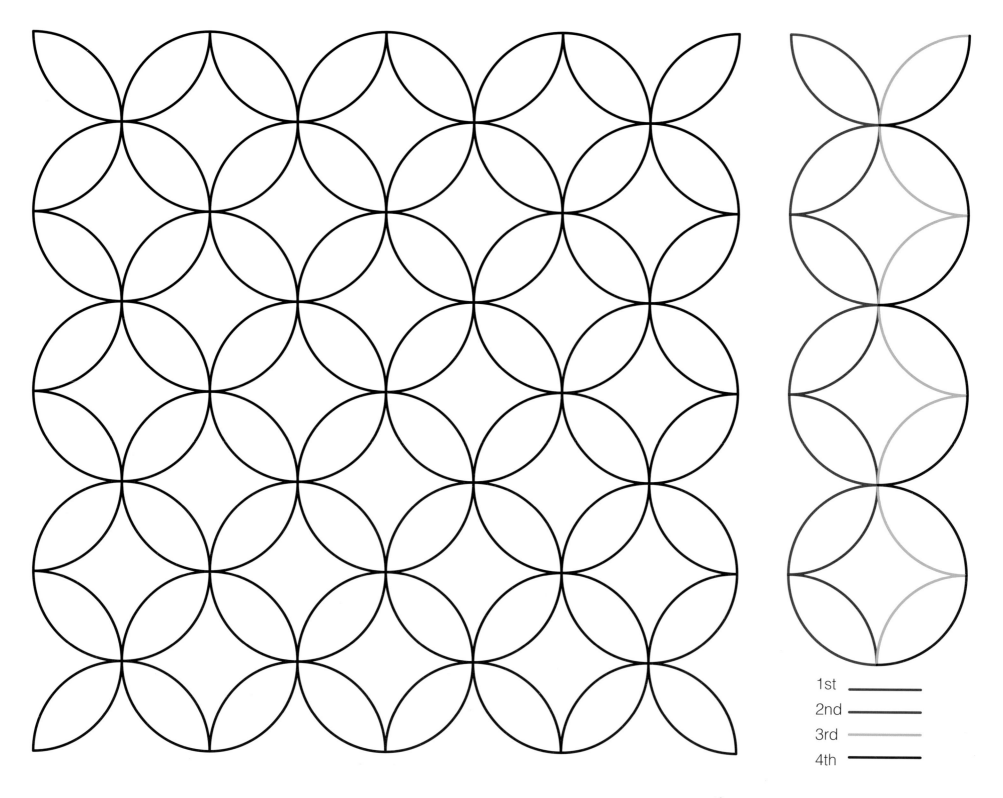

1st ——————
2nd ——————
3rd ——————
4th ——————

Beautiful Quilts as You Go – *Keryn Emmerson*

1st ——————
2nd ——————
3rd ——————
4th ——————

Page 68

About the Author

As a drafter of survey plans and shop drawings on the computer, Keryn Emmerson adapted these skills in designing her own quilting patterns. Residing in Queensland, Australia, Keryn travels to cities and outback areas all over her country to teach machine quilting. Keryn empowers new quilters by teaching many of her projects and patterns using a walking foot. She specializes in longarm quilting patterns and shows students that they can quilt wonderful patterns no matter what their skill level. Keryn employs modern, timesaving methods to make traditional quilts. The first *Golden Threads* designer, she has offered her packets and pantographs to quilters in the United States since 1996.

Other ◆A◆S Books

This is only a small selection of the books available from the American Quilter's Society. AQS books are known worldwide for timely topics, clear writing, beautiful color photos, and for accurate illustrations and patterns. The following books are available from your local bookseller or quilt shop.

The Best of Shirley Thompson QUILTING PATTERNS
Compiled by Cheryl Barnes

#6571   12" x 9" us$24.95

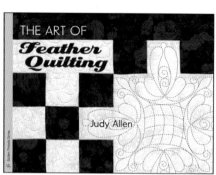

THE ART OF Feather Quilting
Judy Allen

#6678   12" x 9" us$22.95

QUILT SAVVY
Hand Quilting
Virginia "Rusty" Hedrick

#6294
4¼" x 11
us$21.95

Helen's Mix & Match QUILTING PATTERNS
Helen Squire

#6800   us$22.95

Helen's Copy & Use Quilting Patterns
HELEN SQUIRE

#6006   us$25.95

Pathways to Better Quilting
5 shapes for machine quilt patterns
SALLY TERRY

#6509   12" x 9" us$22.95

Diane Gaudynski
GUIDE to MACHINE QUILTING

#6070   us$24.95

Add-a-Line Continued MORE Continuous QUILTING Patterns
Janie Donaldson

#6419   12" x 9" us$24.95

Add-a-Line Continuous QUILTING Patterns
Janie Donaldson

#6069   12" x 9" us$24.95

LOOK for these books nationally.
CALL 1-800-626-5420 or **VISIT** our
Web Site at **www.AmericanQuilter.com**

◆G◆ Products

COMPANION PATTERN PACKS FROM THE AUTHORS WHO WROTE THE BOOKS!

Ready-to-use individual 11" x 17" sheets
of selected patterns in a variety of real sizes.

- Designs • How-to Advice • Popular Motifs

PLUS Bonus Materials

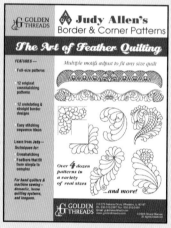

GOLDEN THREADS
Judy Allen's Border & Corner Patterns
The Art of Feather Quilting

#32013   us$16.95

GOLDEN THREADS
Shirley Thompson ◆ QUILTING PATTERNS
Continuous Block & Border Sets

#32012   us$16.95

Quilter's Assistant Proportional Scale

#35023 . . . .$5.95

Golden Threads Quilting Paper
Trace and Sew Tear-Away Stencils

#32001 12" x 20 yds. $7.50
#32002 18" x 20 yds. $10.95
#32003 24" x 20 yds. $12.95

Available at quilt shops, fabric stores, catalogs, or order direct

GOLDEN THREADS
www.goldenthreads.com